inside gymnastics

inside gymnastics

ed gagnier

**drawings by
jack h. bender**

Contemporary Books, Inc.
Chicago

Library of Congress Cataloging in Publication Data

Gagnier, Ed, 1936–
  Inside gymnastics.

  Includes index.
  1. Gymnastics.   I. Title.
GV511.G27   1977   796.4′1   77-22019
ISBN 0-8092-8876-1
ISBN 0-8092-8875-3 pbk.

To my wife, Carolyn, with special thanks
for her help on this book.

Published by Contemporary Books, Inc.
180 North Michigan Avenue, Chicago, Illinois 60601
Manufactured in the United States of America
Library of Congress Catalog Card Number: 77-22019
International Standard Book Number: 0-8092-8876-1 (cloth)
                                                    0-8092-8875-3 (paper)

Published simultaneously in Canada by
Beaverbooks
953 Dillingham Road
Pickering, Ontario L1W 1Z7
Canada

contents

preface

When I first started in gymnastics as a boy, I had little idea of what to expect from the sport. But from the very beginning it provided a real challenge. More than any sport I had tried, I found that gymnastics gave me a great feeling of accomplishment. Now, as a coach, I get the same feeling of accomplishment in seeing my students acquire new skills.

Gymnastics is really not as difficult as it looks. In fact, learning gymnastics is as simple as learning any other sport. The progression of gymnastics skills is logical. A novice can learn some tricks on his very first attempt, and, by sticking with fundamentals and learning the proper basic skills, he can continue to master one new movement after another. The most important things you need are a real desire to learn and great determination.

I've often been asked, "Doesn't a person have to be really strong to become a gymnast?" Most people don't realize that the necessary strength is developed gradually as the gymnast progresses from one fundamental movement to another. But even though gymnastics develops strength, you seldom see an over-developed or muscle-bound gymnast. That's because gymnastics also develops flexibility. The agility of a proficient gymnast is a balanced combination of flexibility and strength.

Not every beginning gymnast is flexible at first. But, like strength, flexibility is an acquired trait. It can be developed if the athlete is willing to work with determination. As a coach of both boys' and girls' gymnastics, I've seen many gymnasts fail to reach their real potential due to poor flexibility. Correct execution is so vitally dependent on flexibility that without it a gymnast simply never becomes a champion.

Of course, a person who has natural flexibility is usually more suited to the sport than someone without it. However, the agility expressed in gymnastics routines is not just an inborn trait; it is a characteristic that is developed by hours and days of hard work. To assure proper development, such training should be done under the supervision of a coach.

Starting gymnastics at an early age can definitely be to an athlete's advantage, since children are usually more flexible than people in their teens. Probably the ideal age for both boys and girls is eight years. Starting a serious training program too much earlier can be harmful to muscle growth and bone development.

As an organized sport, gymnastics has great appeal for many youngsters. A gymnast is not usually limited by his size—anyone who can handle his own weight can become a gymnast. Often a boy who is too small for football or too short for basketball will turn to gymnastics and find that his size is now an advantage.

But gymnastics skills are also important assets in other sports. Just learning how to fall properly without injury can be vital to an athlete. And having complete body control can give a person a great deal of personal confidence in any endeavor.

The strength and grace of a gymnast can be yours, if you're willing to work at it. In this book I've tried to give simple, easy-to-follow guidelines to help you. Or maybe you don't want to be a gymnast yourself but are one of the millions of people who are discovering its excitement as a spectator sport. *Inside Gymnastics* will add greatly to your knowledge and thus to your enjoyment of your next gymnastics meet.

To help you understand the sport even more, I've put unfamiliar terms and important words in italics. These terms are defined in the Glossary at the end of the book. Step-by-step diagrams illustrate the important gymnastics movements. I've also provided an appendix that will show you how gymnastics events are judged. I know you'll find this book a useful introduction to one of the most thrilling and fascinating sports in the world.

Ed Gagnier

OLGA KORBUT . . . the famous Russian gymnast, demonstrates amazing hip flexibility in her routine on the balance beam. This kind of agility comes only with years of dedication and practice.

chapter 1
UNDERSTANDING GYMNASTICS

Since my own early learning days, collegiate gymnastics has been streamlined considerably to make it identical to the modern Olympic competitive program. In the modern program there are six all-around events for men *(floor exercise, pommel horse, rings, vaulting, parallel bars,* and *horizontal bar)* and four all-around events for women *(floor exercise, vaulting, balance beam,* and *uneven parallel bars).*

At one time, men and women each competed in as many as 11 separate events. In addition to the above, these events included *tumbling, trampoline, flying rings,* and *club-swinging* for men and women, *even parallel bars* for women, and *rope climbing* for men.

The events that were discontinued were, for the most part, just duplications or variations of the present events. Men's rings, for example, were divided into two different events, *flying rings* and *still rings,* but essentially the same tricks were performed on both. Flying rings have now been

dropped in favor of still rings. It may be difficult to believe, but women also performed on flying rings. Since the event demanded great shoulder strength, women were somewhat limited in their performance. Now rings have been dropped altogether from the women's competitive program.

Another event once used for both men and women was tumbling. Tumbling duplicated many of the movements already performed in floor exercise. So, along with flying rings, tumbling was eventually dropped.

Two events that have disappeared are rope climbing and club swinging.

The most recent event to be discontinued by both men and women is the trampoline. This event continues to be a part of competitive high school gymnastics programs in some states, but at the collegiate level, trampolining has become a separate sport.

Today most of these former events are

THE POMMEL HORSE . . . is generally considered the most difficult event in the men's all-around program. Here three-time NCAA champion Russ Hoffman performs circles on the horse.

still used in the gym as training aids for developing basic tumbling skills. For example, it is much easier to learn a somersault on the trampoline, with its extra springing action, than it is to learn this same trick on the less lively floor mats.

Probably the most significant change in the modern gymnastics program was the substitution of the uneven parallel bars for the even parallel bars in women's competition. This change in equipment indicated a move away from an emphasis on strength, endurance, and muscular movements and toward emphasizing grace, balance, and movements that were more suited to a woman's body structure.

The differences in emphasis between men's and women's gymnastics can be seen in floor exercise, the only remaining event that is still similar in design for men and women. Tumbling elements in floor exercise are demonstrated by both sexes, but women add elements of ballet and perform to music, while men stick primarily to demonstrations of strength, with emphasis on power and daring.

THE OLYMPIC ALL-AROUND

For the internationally minded competitor, the *all-around* program is of special importance because it is the basis for being selected to compete in the Olympic Games.

The all-around program consists of the four events for women and six events for men that I mentioned earlier. In collegiate gymnastics meets, a winner is recognized for the all-around as well as for each apparatus, so in essence the all-around is an extra event. But it is the most important event for the gymnast interested in qualifying for a future international team. United States all-around competitors have an opportunity to represent their country not only in Olympic competition but also in other international events such as the *Pan American Games,* the *World Championships,* and the *World University Games.*

The original purpose behind the all-around program was to provide a set of events that would develop an athlete's total muscular structure. Some gymnasts have physiques that are better suited for the all-around; other gymnasts are more naturally inclined toward one or two events. Particularly in men's gymnastics, the opportunity to specialize has been provided for those athletes.

Approximately four out of five men are trained as *specialists,* while only one out of every five women is encouraged to specialize. The reason that fewer women than men specialize may be that the women's all-around program requires only four events.

Since an international team must be composed entirely of all-around gymnasts, some of our nation's top specialists are not able to qualify for international competition. Fortunately, in most cases we are still represented by our strongest gymnasts, since the all-around athlete is many times the most outstanding competitor on floor exercise, vaulting, high bar, and parallel bars. The events most frequently dominated by specialists are the pommel horse and rings events.

At the high school level the number of all-around competitors on a team varies greatly. In most states each team must be represented by at least one all-around competitor, and some states go so far as to require all a team's gymnasts to work all-around.

In collegiate-level competition, a designated number of gymnasts in each event must be in the all-around.

Since international competitions are only for all-around gymnasts, the number of competitors on a team representing a country is about half the number normally used on a team in American high school or collegiate programs. In these international competitions, six competitors make up the official team. An alternate is sometimes available, but only six gymnasts are actually allowed in competition. The team score, for both men and women, is based on the five best marks in each event. The low score earned by the sixth gymnast in each event is discarded. This system allows a team to suffer one weak performance without damage to the total team score.

The all-around score is the total of the points earned on all events. The highest possible score in each event is 10 points; therefore, the all-around total is 40 points for women and 60 points for men. However, since most international competitions require a set of *compulsory routines* as well as a set of *optional routines,* the number of possible points is actually doubled. A gymnast capable of scoring 72 points in women's competition or 108 points in men's competition (a 9.0 average in both compulsory and optional events) is considered a top prospect for the Olympic team.

The maximum team score for women is 200 points (10 points times five competitors times four events). A session of compulsories doubles this score for a maximum total of 400 points. For men, there is a possible grand total of 600 points.

The six-competitor system is always used for Olympic, World, and Pan-American Games competitions. However, for the World University Games or for dual international competition between countries, the number of competitors on a team may be fewer than six. In these cases, team scores are proportionately lower, depend-

SPLIT-SECOND REACTIONS . . . and extremely accurate timing are needed to perform such difficult movements as the stutz. Here, All-American Bob Roth prepares to regrasp the rails at the end of the movement.

ing upon the number of gymnasts used in each event.

One important clarification concerning the all-around event is that the total all-around score earned by each gymnast is not calculated into the team score. Only the competitive events making up the all-around are used for team points. The all-around score is significant only for the individual gymnast.

DIFFICULT DISMOUNTS . . . such as the double-back somersault demonstrated here take many weeks of practice in a safety belt before a gymnast is proficient enough to perform safely without assistance.

chapter 2
EQUIPMENT

You don't need any special equipment to learn a few basic gymnastics tricks—you can just practice in your backyard. But once you start working out in a gym and competing in meets, you need to be acquainted with the personal equipment, apparatus, and safety equipment that gymnasts use.

PERSONAL EQUIPMENT

Your personal equipment includes clothing for competition and chalk or rosin to prevent slippery hands and feet. Your school or team may provide the personal equipment. But even if you have to buy it yourself, you will find that the outfit required for gymnastics costs much less than the uniforms for most other school sports.

Handguards

The one thing that is most vivid in my mind from my first experiences in gymnastics is how sore and dried out my hands became after each practice. As a rule, fundamental

movements will not cause much stress; but as you work harder on the more difficult tricks, your hands become sore and hot. To cope with this problem, use *handguards,* or *grips,* to provide some protection for your hands.

An experienced gymnast will try to quit working out before his hands get too hot. If you don't stop when you should, you are liable to develop blisters or even a *rip.* A rip, considered more serious than a blister, occurs when a portion of skin is torn from the palm of the hand. A rip isn't too serious, but it does limit a competitor's performance for the next few days. Having callused, hardened hands and wearing handguards will not prevent rips. Handguards allow you to work a little longer, but you still have to know when to quit. Women have problems with rips primarily on the uneven parallel bars. Men must be watchful on the horizontal bar, parallel bars, rings, and pommel horse.

At one time it was quite common for gymnasts to make their own protective handguards from scrap pieces of leather. Today handguards are sold in either leather or a lampwick-type material. Both kinds are equally effective. The handguard a gymnast decides to use generally is a matter of personal preference.

Since grips tend to break in differently on each event, most male gymnasts have several different pairs. Women need only one pair, for the uneven parallel bars. Grip sizes are small, medium, and large. Sizing depends not only on the size of the hand, but also on the event for which they are to be used and the manner in which they are to be worn. Normally a handguard is attached over the middle two fingers, laid over the palm of the hand, and secured firmly around the wrist.

The price of grips varies depending upon the thickness and durability of the material. If you work out daily, you can usually expect two or three months of wear before your handguards break or wear out.

Generally, handguards are not worn by beginning gymnasts. Working fundamental tricks without grips allows your hands to toughen up a little more quickly. You can use handguards more effectively if you've already learned how to grasp the equipment properly. When to begin wearing grips depends on the length of daily workouts and the extent to which you experience hand problems.

It is also important for you to try to retain some degree of softness in your hands between workouts. Since men work more events requiring grips than women, the problem of drying hands is of more concern to men. Usually, applying a moist hand cream between workouts seems to work very well in retaining some moisture in the hands.

Chalk

One absolute necessity for working most events is *chalk,* technically called *magne-*

THE HORIZONTAL BAR . . . puts a great deal of stress on a gymnast's hands. Iowa State gymnast Mike Jacki wears handguards as he performs this event.

sium carbonate. Chalk is necessary for reducing sweating of the hands, thus insuring a firm, secure grip on the apparatus. Apply just enough chalk to keep your hands dry. If you're going to do several tricks or a full routine at once, apply enough chalk to last through the full set of movements. Knowing how much to apply comes with experience.

Rosin

Rosin, used by women primarily on the balance beam, is not to be confused with chalk. Rosin is used only on soles of footwear for better traction. It is never applied directly to the skin. In some cases, rosin is preferred over chalk for better foot traction in vaulting.

Wrist Wraps

In recent years, wrist wraps have become more popular. They serve the dual purpose of providing wrist support and protecting the wrists from the sharp pulling action of the handguards. The grips can be attached comfortably over the wrist wraps. Wrist wraps can be made of different materials. Most gymnasts use a narrow, two-inch, ribbing material wrapped several times around the wrist and anchored with athletic tape. A simple knit wrist warmer or an elastic snap-on wrist warmer that can be purchased from the drugstore may also be used.

Footwear

With all the twisting and somersaulting you do in gymnastics, the type of footwear you use is very important. Gymnastics shoes should be light. There is no sense in you carrying around extra weight. Of equal importance is that slippers must not hinder your efforts to demonstrate proper form. Therefore, they should be reasonably soft and pliable. Men and women use the same kind of footwear in competition.

Gymnastics slippers are made from soft leather or canvas. A good pair will last from six months to a year. A substitute for slippers is simply a pair of socks or anklets, or lowcut nylon stretch foot socks that are normally worn inside street shoes. Since you are in the air or around soft mats most of the time, even light weight anklets hold up very well. One advantage to wearing socks or anklets is that they make it easier to show better foot form on the equipment. One disadvantage is that they do not provide the same positive foot traction as slippers. On events such as vaulting and floor exercise, you might wear slippers to gain better traction, and use more form-fitted socks or anklets on other events that do not require as much jumping.

Hair Holders

Turning somersaults makes your hair fly in every direction. If you have long hair, this can become quite a problem. Take special precautions to wear a proper hairstyle. For practice, it is usually sufficient to hold long hair firmly behind the head with a rubber band. For more formal competitions, many women gymnasts choose a hairstyle in which the hair is held firmly toward the top of the head. For those with shorter hair, ponytails seem to do just as well. Proper hairstyles not only look better during competition but add to personal safety—getting your hair caught while executing a movement can be extremely painful and dangerous.

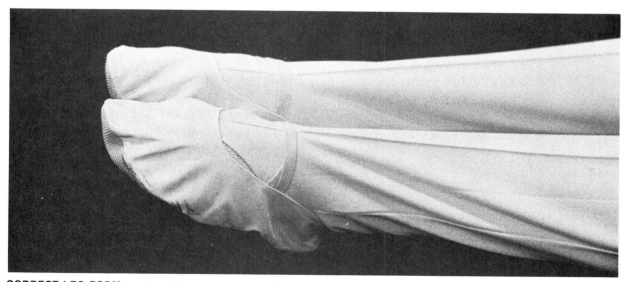

CORRECT LEG FORM . . . is accentuated by spanking- white trousers and slippers. The correct form consists of holding the legs straight and firmly together, with the feet and toes pointed.

Uniforms

A clean, properly fitting uniform is the pride of any gymnast. Competitive gymnastics uniforms are tailored to complement the proper execution of a gymnast's performance. Men's trousers are tapered to improve the extended effect when the feet are pointed. The advantage of the traditional white trousers is that they do not show chalk smudges. In the past, international tradition required the gymnast to wear a white shirt top as well as white trousers. However, wearing bright-colored shirts representing the country or school colors is now more common. The competition shirt is long enough to be securely fastened under the crotch to prevent the shirt from slipping upward.

Because of the endless variety of body motions that are carried out, the shirt and trousers must be made of a two-way stretch material. Suspenders and elastic foot stirrups help to hold the trousers properly.

The women's competitive uniform is a leotard. Like men's shirt tops, the leotards used in competition are colorful and creative in design. Sleeves can be varied in length to suit a gymnast's desires. The leotard is made of a two-way stretch material. For the mature and advanced gymnast, tailored leotards are always preferred. Stockings are very seldom worn.

Warmup suits (jacket tops and long trousers) are basically the same for men and women. Well-fitted jackets and tapered pants to emphasize leg form assure complete freedom of movement while performing.

APPARATUS

With the proper personal equipment, you're now ready to be introduced to the gym equipment you will use.

Floor Mat

The floor mat is used by both men and

FLOOR MAT.

women. The standard floor mat is square: 39 feet, 4½ inches on each side. The mat must be at least one inch thick. Years ago floor exercise was performed on the bare floor, which offered no protection whatsoever. Now a gymnast enjoys a smooth protective surface. A mat also provides added spring to somersaults. However, the surface cannot be too soft, since a surface lacking in firmness would be very hard to balance on during such movements as handstands.

In an effort to maintain the firmness desired but still provide protection, a recent trend has been to cover the floor mat with a carpet. This not only makes the surface more attractive but it adds comfort and quietness. Because the nap of the carpet is extremely short, any danger of unsure footing is nearly nonexistent.

Except for its carpet cover, the gymnastics mat is almost identical to the surface used for amateur competitive wrestling. In fact, it is very common for wrestlers and gymnasts to share the same mat as a means of keeping down expenses.

The cost of a floor exercise mat varies depending upon its features. The less expensive models usually have to be disas-

POMMEL HORSE.

sembled completely in order to be moved, whereas the higher-priced mats will fold into a single unit ready for storage.

In order to provide an added margin of safety, the floor exercise mat is made about 2 feet larger than regulation. A 2-inch-wide line marks the official competitive area.

Pommel Horse

Originally, a pommel horse body had four legs and even a tail. Today the tail has been eliminated, the overall length has been shortened to a more workable size, and the pommels are made of wood or synthetic material, instead of steel castings covered with leather. European horse bodies are still supported by four wooden legs, but even this is changing in favor of the more modern two-legged supports used in the United States. The horse body is padded and covered with leather. The pommels that extend 5 inches above the horse body can be adjusted in width to suit each gymnast.

The horse body is 63 to 64 inches long. International regulations call for the horse to be set at a height of $43^5/_{16}$ inches from the floor for pommel horse events. American pommel horses are set a little higher

(45¼ inches) to accommodate our taller gymnasts. Since adjusting the pommels can be bothersome, most gymnasts prefer to have them set at the standard width of about 17 inches. The horse is placed in the middle of a 12- by 12-foot mat that is 3¼ inches thick.

Vaulting Equipment

For vaulting events, the pommels on the horse are removed. For men's vaulting, the horse's height is raised to 53 inches. The height for women's vaulting is 47¼ inches. In competition, women vault over the width, and men over the length of the horse body.

An important piece of equipment for vaulting is a springboard, which is placed on the floor. To provide better foot traction, a rubber runner (mat) is extended under the board and along the length of the runway.

The landing mats are positioned at the opposite end of the horse. Adequate mat protection is particularly important because of the sudden stop that is essential after each vault. As an additional protective measure, a 1-inch-thick pad is placed on top of the springboard to soften the

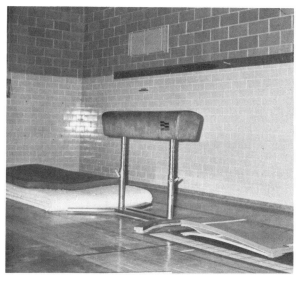

VAULTING APPARATUS . . . includes the horse without its pommels, plus a springboard and landing mats.

abrupt jarring action during takeoff. The springboard is not designed to be especially powerful. Although the board is capable of yielding a moderate lift, its purpose is to provide a cushioning action for the feet during the hard takeoff.

RINGS.

Rings

Competitive equipment for rings can be assembled in one of two ways. The method most often used for high school competition is to hang the rings from cables attached to ceiling beams in the gymnasium. Not as simple to install, but much more dramatic in effect, is the method of attaching rings from a metal *rings frame*. This latter method is required for collegiate competition. An important advantage of a rings frame is that it can be used in large arenas.

The rings frame flexes slightly, which is an advantage for the performer. Also, the competitor experiences a comfortable awareness of the equipment that is not possible on rings hung from the ceiling.

Ceiling-mounted rings can be installed for considerably less than the type hung from a rings frame.

There are only two crucial height specifi-

cations for rings. The upper cable assemblies must be attached 18 feet, 4 inches above the floor, while the wooden rings hang with a clearance of 102 inches above the floor. At this height, a gymnast can hang by his hands and swing without hitting his feet on the floor.

Mats are required in the landing area directly beneath the rings. A taller competitor in danger of scraping his feet on the mat may reduce the thickness accordingly. However, it is rather uncommon for a gymnast to be that tall.

Parallel Bars

Originally, parallel bar rails were stiff and added very little to a performance. The modern wooden or fiberglass rails are more flexible. The spring action provided by these more elastic rails not only makes the parallel bars more comfortable for the gymnast but also allows the gymnast to develop more height on each trick.

Each rail measures 11 feet, 6 inches in length. The rails are oval, with an average thickness of 2 inches. Adjusting the width and height of the rails is of critical importance. On the parallel bars, unlike most

PARALLEL BARS.

events, it is necessary to make adjustments to suit the height of each competitor, to allow a gymnast the freedom to hang on the rails by his upper arms while still being up high enough to clear the floor with his feet.

The width between the bars may also be adjusted. Most competitors tend to work a common height of 5½ feet; however, individual width preferences will vary between 17 and 19 inches.

For safety, mats are placed around the bars and beneath the rails. If the gymnast desires, he is allowed to use a springboard for mounting the equipment.

Uneven Parallel Bars

In women's gymnastics the uneven parallel bars are used instead of the parallel bars. The uneven bars are designed better to suit the female body structure. The uprights supporting the two rails are either attached to a heavy portable base or anchored to the floor with steel cables. The bars, made of wood or fiberglass are designed to be flexible. Fiberglass rails tend to be more elastic than wood. The distance between the bars must be properly adjusted to suit each gymnast. This measurement varies slightly with each gymnast. When a gymnast is swinging from a hanging position on the upper bar her hips must contact the low bar at just the right spot. For most gymnasts this spot is right at the bending point in the hips. Proper contact allows more comfort and prevents an abrupt jarring action as the body is swung into and around the low bar.

Mats are placed beneath the rails and on both sides of the bars in order to provide adequate protection for *dismounts* performed in either direction. A springboard may also be provided to give the gymnast a more explosive start.

Horizontal Bar (High Bar)

The apparatus for the high bar event is a solid steel bar 94½ inches long and 1 1/10

inches in diameter. The bar is 102 inches off the floor. It is supported by vertical uprights with cables anchored to floor plates.

The steel bar is amazingly flexible. It is very common to see a bar bend 3 or 4 inches under the weight of each movement made by the performer. With amazing accuracy, the bar always returns to its original straight position. In my 28 years in gymnastics, I've never seen a bar bend to the point of breaking. Of course, it does happen, but only rarely.

The high bar is centered over a mat. Specially designed landing mats that extend out in both directions can be adjusted to suit the individual competitor. The landing mats are often spread apart under the bar to allow a gymnast more clearance for his feet.

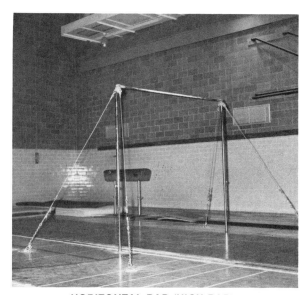

HORIZONTAL BAR (HIGH BAR).

Balance Beam

Only 3⁵⁄₁₆ inches wide, the balance beam provides barely enough room for a comfortable footing. It is 16 feet, 4⅞ inches long and is set 47¼ inches above the ground. This elevation offers sufficient clearance for a gymnast to swing her legs down while in a sitting position. The height has also

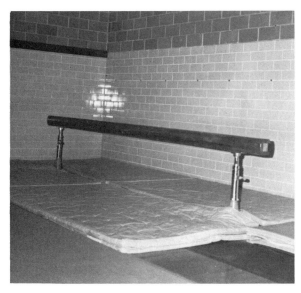

BALANCE BEAM.

proved ideal for demonstrating a challenging *mount* or spectacular dismount. The entire structure is supported by stable uprights capable of restraining any undesirable movements of the apparatus.

International authorities on specifications have recently been experimenting with placing a thin, soft, padded cover over the entire surface of the balance beam. Padding of a slightly thicker material is placed on the top surface in order to reduce the hard landings that occur after high leaping and tumbling movements. Preliminary findings indicate that official acceptance of such padding is definitely expected in the near future.

For safety, a beam is surrounded by mats on both sides and on each end.

SAFETY EQUIPMENT

I'm sure many people have wondered how a gymnast goes about learning new and seemingly daring gymnastics movements. Well, let me set your mind at ease right now—there is little or no danger for the gymnast who takes advantage of the proper safety devices available.

Safety Belt

Probably the most popular safety device for learning difficult new stunts is the *safety belt,* which supports a gymnast by means of ropes hung from ceiling beam pulleys and attached around the performer's waist. The other end of the rope is held by the coach or spotter who provides the necessary assistance, even to the extent of holding the gymnast completely free of the floor. When learning a movement, a gymnast uses a safety belt of this type until the movement has been completely mastered to the satisfaction of both the gymnast and the coach.

THE SAFETY BELT . . . is the safest method for learning a new movement. I find this system of spotting especially useful when a performer's motion rises too high for me to use the hand-spotting method.

Crash Pads

Even when a safety belt is no longer needed, other safety devices can be substituted until the gymnast can perform the movement without any assistance at all. Large, thick, soft landing mats, or *crash pads* as they are more popularly called, provide a safe landing area if the gymnast should make an error and land on his back.

Hand Spotting

When attempting some movement on

THE CRASH PAD . . . provides a soft, safe landing when a gymnast misses a difficult trick.

A HAND SPOT . . . is the quickest, surest way of providing assistance. I can employ this method on any movement in which the gymnast's motion remains within my reach.

which neither a safety belt nor a crash pad can be used, the gymnast can usually be guided by the *hand spotting* techniques employed by a knowledgeable coach.

It should be pointed out that a gymnast cannot expect to master a new stunt the first time around no matter what safety device is employed. Learning some movements just seems to take time and practice. The speed at which learning takes place depends on how physically and mentally prepared the gymnast is.

THE STAG HANDSTAND . . . as performed here by Olga Korbut on the balance beam, is a variation of the basic handstand movement.

chapter 3
THE BASIC DOZEN

Whether you're 8 or 18, you should begin gymnastics with the fundamentals. Fortunately, the basic movements of gymnastics don't require special apparatus. If a tumbling mat is available, go ahead and use it, but a soft, smooth lawn will do just as well.

You don't need a special uniform. An old pair of shorts and a shirt will do fine. Just kick your shoes off and you're ready to go.

For the most part these movements are performed about as close to the ground as you can get, so you don't have to be too concerned about falling and getting hurt.

Begin by mastering the following 12 basic skills. Once learned on the ground, these same tricks can be transferred to the apparatus in a variety of ways. Attain reasonable success with the first move before going on to the next. A movement learned on the ground can be transferred to the apparatus with amazing quickness. In a very simple sense, gymnastics is nothing more than tumbling on the equipment.

FRONT TUCK ROLL

The purpose of the *front tuck roll* (Diagram 1) is to provide experience in turning over 360 degrees. During the process of turning over, avoid stopping halfway around or leaning to one side. To a certain extent, you are also learning to balance as your body turns over.

Bend your knees to a squat position. Place your hands on the ground about 18 inches in front of your feet. Keep your wrists about shoulder-distance apart and point your fingers straight ahead. Now straighten your legs and push your body forward in a rolling motion over your head.

In order to make the rolling action over the head as smooth as possible, tuck your head in tight against your chest, allowing the weight of your body to rest on your hands and shoulders. Halfway through the roll, as your weight rolls toward your hips, place your hands on the floor and pull your feet tightly in next to your seat. This hard

DIAGRAM 1. The front tuck roll.

tucking action helps you roll forward to a standing position.

At times you may have trouble rolling all the way up. If this is the case, push off your feet a little harder in the beginning to gain the necessary momentum.

BACK TUCK ROLL

Like the forward tuck roll, the *back tuck roll* helps you develop your *air sense* as you turn over 360 degrees. But this time you will roll backwards (Diagram 2).

Squat down and place your hands on the floor slightly behind your feet. As your weight shifts backwards over your hips and shoulders, move your hands and place them behind your shoulders next to your ears. As your weight is transferred to your head, push yourself up to a squatting position and then straighten up.

Rolling backwards requires more arm push than rolling forward, so be prepared to push as hard as possible. If you tend to stop when you get only halfway over, make the following adjustments. First, roll backwards a little faster; second, make every effort to stay in a small tuck, immediately placing your feet on the floor behind your head. Staying in a small ball or *tucked position* as you roll over will allow you to complete this trick in a smooth manner.

BACK STRADDLE ROLL

Once you have mastered the back tuck roll, the *back straddle roll* is very simple to execute. The main difference is that your legs are spread apart and straight (Diagram 3).

Begin this movement in a standing position with your feet about 30 inches apart. Reach down between your legs, placing your hands on the floor behind your feet. Now sit back by supporting your weight with your hands. As your weight begins to shift from your hips to the back of your shoulders, place your hands on the floor behind your shoulders as you did in the back tuck roll. Continue the rolling action, keeping your body in a *pike position* and placing your feet, which are still spread apart on the floor, directly behind your head. As your weight shifts to your feet, push yourself to an upright position with your hands and arms.

DIAGRAM 2. The back tuck roll.

DIAGRAM 3. The back straddle roll.

As in the back tuck roll, it is important not to open the body to a straight position during the roll. This straightening action will tend to slow you down completely. One key point is to place your feet on the floor behind your head as soon as possible. And remember—it is going to take a good strong push with your hands and arms to stand up.

FRONT STRADDLE ROLL

By combining the techniques learned from the first three fundamental movements, you can now perform the *front straddle roll* successfully (Diagram 4). You need more hip flexibility for this trick than in the three you have already learned.

Stand with your feet about 30 inches apart. Lean forward and place your hands on the floor. Keeping your head tucked against your chest, bend your arms and roll forward, allowing the weight of your body to settle on the back of your shoulders. As your weight continues to shift forward toward your hips, keep your legs straight and spread as wide as possible. Here's where good flexibility comes in. As you approach a sitting position on the floor, your hands should be placed on the floor between your legs. By keeping your legs spread as wide as possible, push yourself forward and upward with your hands to the original standing straddle position.

If you have difficulty in rolling up, it is no doubt due to your inability to keep your legs spread wide enough. In completing the roll, make every effort to push as hard as possible with your hands. Don't make the mistake of giving up too early.

HEAD BALANCE

You've probably tried standing on your head at one time or other. The secret to a good *head balance* (Diagram 5) is keeping your weight distributed evenly between your hands and head.

Squat down, placing your hands on the floor about a foot in front of your feet. The position of your hands is quite important. Place your hands shoulder-distance apart, with your fingers pointing outward. Now bend your arms and place your head on the floor about a foot in front of your hands. By pressing down with your hands, raise your hips to a vertical position over your head. When you feel you are balanced, draw your legs off the floor in a tuck against your body. Once you feel secure in the tucked head balance position, slowly extend your legs to a vertical position. Try to keep your body as straight as possible.

One of the first mistakes made by most people who attempt the head balance is failing to place the head on the floor far enough in front of the hands. Forming a balanced triangle with the hands and head

DIAGRAM 4. The front straddle roll.

DIAGRAM 5. The head balance.

is most important. Keep your weight equally distributed. Too much weight on the head will cause you to fall over. Too much weight on the hands makes it difficult to get up to the balanced position. Hold your head and neck muscles firm. You have found the proper contact point if you feel your weight on the front top part of your head.

FRONT SCALE

The *front scale* (Diagram 6) is one of the most basic balance positions in gymnastics. Learning to balance on one foot is not very difficult, but attaining the correct position, which calls for a high degree of flexibility, can be very challenging.

Which foot to balance on is a matter of personal preference. For the competitive gymnast it is an advantage to be able to execute the scale on either foot.

From a standing position, begin raising one leg backward until it is approximately 12 inches off the ground. At this point, check to be certain that you have your body arched from the tip of your foot to the top of your head. While maintaining this technically correct arched position, continue raising your leg backward and upward as high as possible. As your leg raises higher, it will be necessary to lower your upper body forward and downward to maintain proper balance. In the final position, hold

DIAGRAM 6. The front scale.

your foot slightly higher than your head. During the movement your arms can be held in different positions. In competition, arm position depends on how the scale fits into the rest of your routine.

HANDSTAND

The ability to execute a good, solid *handstand* (Diagram 7) should be the primary objective of any young, would-be gymnast. I can't think of any movement more characteristic of gymnastics. Don't be too surprised if it takes a little time to learn this trick. Your control and balance will continue to improve with years of experience in the sport.

Bend forward, placing your hands on the floor, shoulder-width apart, about 18 inches in front of your feet. Spread your fingers, making a good solid base. Point them straight ahead. At this stage, check that your elbows are straight and that your shoulders are directly over your fingertips. Leaning forward with the shoulders is very important. Most people fail to lean forward far enough. Keep your head up, with your eyes looking forward toward your fingertips.

Now you are in the proper position to kick to a handstand. With one leg placed slightly ahead of the other, kick the back leg into a position like the one in the scale. Keep going until you're doing a handstand. When your back leg nears the vertical position, your second leg should join it. At this point your body should be as straight as possible. Only a slight arch is acceptable; too much of an arch is incorrect.

Maintaining balance requires keeping your shoulders forward (over your fingertips) and making minor adjustments with your fingers by pressing against the ground. Avoid the bad habits of bending your elbows or piking your hips.

Coming down smoothly from a handstand can be just as difficult as getting up. If possible, try to come back down on one

DIAGRAM 7. The handstand.

foot, reversing the manner used to go up. Avoid coming down with two feet together, since it can cause you to stub your toes. If you lose your balance and fall over, simply bend your arms, duck your head, and perform a front tuck roll.

When you first start doing handstands, have someone hold your legs, or practice kicking to a handstand against a flat wall. I have also encouraged my young beginners to walk on their hands, since learning how to stay upside down can be accomplished more quickly if the gymnast is allowed to walk in order to keep balanced. However, the main objective eventually will be to balance in one spot without any movement, and this takes time and patience.

CARTWHEEL

The *cartwheel* (Diagram 8) is probably the gymnastics skill most often attempted by interested beginners. Some people are able to learn the cartwheel right away, while others are slow to sense the correct position, even when spotted by a coach.

First, establish an imaginary straight line on the ground in the direction you intend to cartwheel. Now stand on one end of this imaginary line. Kick your left leg forward and upward while turning your body slightly to the right. As you lower your left leg to the floor, raise both arms sideways and in a circling action, leaning your upper body forward and down along the imaginary line. Reaching down with both hands, place your left hand and your right on the line. Just as your hands contact the floor kick your right leg vigorously overhead, drawing your left leg behind it. When passing through the vertical position, keep your legs straight and spread apart as wide as possible. Your right leg should pass over your head in a continuous motion and come down on the imaginary line just beyond your right hand. As your body continues to cartwheel, push your left and right hands off the floor and circle up to a sideways position as you lower your left leg to the floor beyond the right leg.

In order to perform a technically correct cartwheel, your body must travel through a

DIAGRAM 8. The cartwheel.

vertical plane over your hands. Failing to move the legs directly overhead during the first few attempts is perfectly normal. However, you must continue to try to make the legs pass directly overhead. The cartwheel is easier to execute if you keep your legs as wide as possible while turning over. One more point: Keep watching your hands as they push off from the floor. Looking at your hands will prevent any extra twisting action that interferes with the proper landing position of your feet.

BACK EXTENSION ROLL

The *back extension roll* (Diagram 9) is basically a continuation of the back tuck roll you learned earlier. You will now combine two movements, the back tuck roll and the handstand.

Begin from a standing position. Circle both arms down to the floor behind the feet. Leaning backwards with legs straight, lower your body to the floor with your hands. From this sitting position, continue to roll backwards, drawing your legs overhead in a deep piked position. While your legs are passing over your face, place your hands beside your ears under your shoulders as you did in the back tuck roll. With your hands placed palms down, firmly push with your arms while simultaneously snapping your body open to a straight handstand position. Then lower your legs to the floor one at a time.

The most critical part of this trick is coordinating the push of the arms with the snapping open of the body. As with a great number of gymnastics moves, timing is of utmost importance. Another point to remember is to bring the legs into a good piked position close to the face before snapping out. This deep pike will allow you to snap with more force and guidance.

FRONT LIMBER

The *front limber* (Diagram 10) can be learned quickly by a gymnast with good back flexibility.

From a standing position, kick up to a handstand. Once in a handstand, allow your back to arch as much as possible while falling over to your feet. As your feet land on the floor, keep your head up with your eyes looking toward your feet. At this point the weight of your body should be transferred quickly from your hands to your feet. Keeping your back in as big an arch as possible, move back up to an erect position.

It is important to arch your body as much as possible while you are still in a handstand position. The more arch you achieve, the closer your feet will be placed

DIAGRAM 9. The back extension roll.

DIAGRAM 10. The front limber.

on the floor next to your hands. Also, when you attempt to stand up, be sure to look back and to keep your arms outstretched overhead. This position of your head and arms not only helps you to stand up smoothly but also lets you use your hands in case you are not able to get all the way up to a standing position. As I mentioned earlier, the most critical requirement for this trick is good back flexibility.

BACK LIMBER

The *back limber* is almost identical to the front limber except that the procedure is done in reverse (Diagram 11). Having a good flexible back will again be to your advantage.

From a standing position, arch your back as much as possible, maintaining a balanced position on your feet. By raising your arms in a circular movement overhead, lean your body back, placing your hands on the floor as close to your heels as possible. Some beginners prefer to execute this first phase of the trick from a kneeling position. Being a little closer to the floor usually makes you a little more confident.

Keeping your arms straight, shift your weight from your feet to your hands. By moving your hips and shoulders forward over your hands, raise your legs off the

ground to a handstand position and on to the floor again in one circular motion. It is usually helpful for the beginner to push off the floor with the feet in order to complete the last phase of the trick.

FRONT HEADSPRING

By combining the initial phase of the front tuck roll, the pushing and snapping action of the back extension roll, and the arching action of the front limber, you can perform a *front headspring* (Diagram 12) with amazing ease.

From a standing position, squat down and place your hands on the floor about 18 inches in front of your feet, as you did in the front tuck roll. As soon as your hands touch the floor, push off with your feet while lowering your head until it just touches the floor. Do not rest too much weight on your head, but try to support as much weight as possible on your hands. As your legs rise off the floor, keep your knees as straight as possible. Bend 90 degrees at your hips, forming an inverted L. From this inverted-L position, allow your hips to continue moving forward over your head. After your hips have passed over your head, push vigorously with the arms while simultaneously snapping the body open from the inverted-L position to an arched position.

DIAGRAM 11. The back limber.

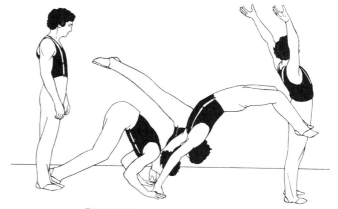

DIAGRAM 12. The front headspring.

In snapping to the arched position, direct your feet toward the floor. With constant momentum, a good push, and a complete snap to an arch, you will land on your feet in a standing position.

Failure to complete the headspring is usually a result of snapping and pushing too early. A little extra momentum, gained from pushing extra hard with the feet, is usually also helpful.

It takes time and patience to learn new gymnastics skills. But there is consolation in the fact that once a trick is properly mastered it is never forgotten. Be prepared to spend a reasonable amount of time on each of these tricks. Some movements will require more effort and patience than others. If you apply yourself, each different trick will be a new and enjoyable experience.

A SCALE . . . requires
flexibility as well as
balance.

THE CARTWHEEL BACK SOMERSAULT . . . requires a particularly explosive takeoff and a high degree of air sense. Big-8 conference champion Stew Buck executes the tuck portion of the movement.

chapter 4
MEN'S EVENTS

Within each of the six competitive events of men's gymnastics, there are literally hundreds of different movements possible. But each of these movements, no matter how complicated it seems, can be broken down into simple, logical steps that are based on previously learned movements. If you train with determination under the supervision of a good coach, you'll soon progress from the basic tricks of the last chapter to the more complex movements I will describe in this chapter.

If you are a spectator, study the diagrams in this and the next chapter as well as the Appendix on judging. Learning the names of the key movements and knowing the standards by which judges evaluate the events will greatly increase your enjoyment of meets.

Although each athlete has a different style and body build, there is only one "correct" postural style for each event. The correct technical execution is often referred to as the *international style.*

Before competing in an event, a gymnast works out a *routine,* a logical, personal combination of movements. His objective is to devise a routine that will earn him the highest possible number of points. Each gymnast must fulfill certain requirements in each event.

Once a gymnast establishes his routine, he makes as few deviations from it as he can. Under no circumstances would an experienced competitor attempt a routine in competition without first having the entire sequence of tricks in mind. Only under pressure of an error would he execute an unplanned movement.

In this chapter I will discuss the requirements and key elements of skill for each of the six events only in reference to optional routines. Important open championships, collegiate conference championships, NCAA championships, and the Olympic Games also require a set of compulsory routines. In the evaluation of *compulsories,* the difficulty of the exercise is not taken into consideration. Since all gymnasts perform the same compulsory exercises on each event, combination factors are also disregarded. In compulsories, the only factor evaluated is execution. The main purpose of a compulsory exercise is to put all the competitors on equal ground in an effort to evaluate more accurately each man's ability to execute movements correctly. In the optional routines, when judges have the added responsibility of evaluating *difficulty* and *combination* (the structure of the routine), execution is often overlooked. But the gymnast capable of displaying the best compulsory routine will generally be capable of one of the best performances in the optional routines.

A gymnast is allowed only one attempt on each event. A gymnast who loses hold of the equipment is allowed to remount and continue his routine, with a 0.50 points reduction in his score.

FLOOR EXERCISE

A floor exercise performance lasts longer and demands more total physical exertion than any of the other five men's events. The ability to perform satisfactorily in floor exercise seems to have little to do with the size of the gymnast. The overall physical endurance of the competitor is more important than size.

Floor exercise is based primarily on straight tumbling sequences. Fast, high-tumbling somersaults will always earn handsome scores. A gymnast should not look heavy and awkward on landings, be rough and jerky in his movements, or lack control and balance in *hold positions*. He must move smoothly, be light on his feet, and perform in a confident, controlled manner. His main objective is to make a difficult trick look easy.

Evaluation

In his floor exercise routine, a gymnast must fulfill an *11-part requirement* (one trick of superior difficulty, five tricks of intermediate difficulty, and five tricks of lower difficulty). Rules specify that the floor exercise routine should be "harmoniously rhythmical." A gymnast must alternate movements of balance with *hold parts,* leaps, *kips,* tumbling sequences, and a strength part.

The judges begin the process of evaluation as soon as a gymnast starts his first pass. In United States collegiate competitions, a gymnast can perform without the pressure of a time limit. International rules, on the other hand, dictate a time limit of between 50 and 70 seconds. Since deductions are made for going over or under the time limits, a bell or buzzer system is used to alert the gymnast and judges of the minimum and maximum limits. Since almost all routines will be close to 60 seconds in duration, the added expenses and arrangements of a timer have seemed unnecessary to American officials.

Beginning Your Routine

After you receive a starting signal from the head judge, approach the mat and walk directly to your selected starting point. Rules allow you to begin your routine from any spot on the mat. You may not start your first pass outside the official area. Make every attempt to avoid getting too close to the boundary line. Stepping over or even touching the line will result in a reduction of your score.

Most gymnasts elect to begin their routines from one corner of the mat. Tumbling down the diagonal offers more running room to initiate the first pass. You will usually *mount* (perform your first trick or sequence of tricks) with your most impressive and difficult movements, so you will probably prefer the extra running room on the diagonal.

Covering the Area

In order to discourage too many diagonal passes, the rules require you to make use of the entire mat area. The most common floor pattern is to use two diagonal passes, one pass down the side, and a fourth pass down the second diagonal in completing the *dismount*. Some gymnasts will attempt even more creative ways of covering the entire area. However, this simple floor pattern fulfills the requirements that you touch all four corners of the mat.

Transitions

After you complete your first pass, you must perform certain moves in the corner to change direction. These tricks are called *transitions*. In most instances these are movements of lower difficulty. A more proficient gymnast will attempt to insert transitions of intermediate or superior difficulty whenever possible.

Transitions can be an area for major deductions. Most transitions are of low-difficulty value, so a gymnast with unsure footing or poor body motion can lose many points while gaining little or no points for risk. Besides turning the gymnast around, the primary purpose of a transition is to add more interest and creative continuity to the routine.

Tumbling Movements

Most tumbling movements are variations of the somersaulting movements you learned in the last chapter. You build on these basic movements to put together more complicated maneuvers. And, as I mentioned earlier, you can transfer many of the skills you learn for floor exercise to other events.

In gymnastics, a somersault is often called a *flip* or simply referred to by its descriptive title, as in the *double back,* when the double somersaulting action is implied.

An important element of all tumbling movements is *height*. Height is usually demonstrated at the end of a tumbling sequence. Use the preliminary movements, such as the *round-off* and the *back handspring,* to build enough momentum for the high somersault at the end of a pass. Because physical body structure prevents a gymnast from tumbling forward as efficiently as he tumbles backwards, back somersaults have much more height than forward somersaults.

Ratings for the various tumbling movements reflect their level of difficulty. Single forward or backward somersaults (Diagrams 13 and 14) are considered movements of intermediate difficulty. Usually any flip that contains a half-twist or more is

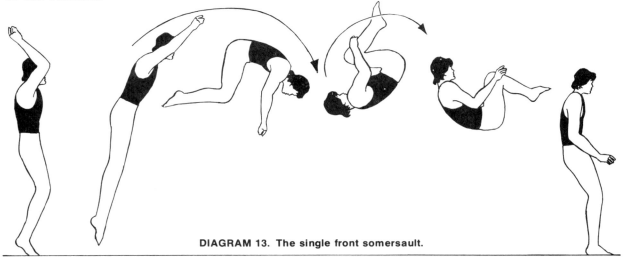

DIAGRAM 13. The single front somersault.

DIAGRAM 14. The single back somersault. This somersault can be executed in the layout, pike, or tuck positions.

given a superior rating.

Seldom will a gymnast turn over more than 1½ times (Diagram 15) or execute more than one full twist when tumbling forward. Therefore, both of these tricks are in the superior category. One of the most spectacular tumbling tricks is the *double-back somersault* (Diagram 16). This trick contains two full flips. It must be executed with as much explosive height as possible.

This trick requires exceptional strength as well as the ability to tumble in an explosive, high manner.

A *double full-twisting somersault* (Diagram 17) is also considered a superior movement. The double full contains two full twists and a flip. Although not as difficult as the double back, the double-full is nonetheless a stunt of considerable difficulty. The double back and double full are

DIAGRAM 15. The one and one half front somersault.

DIAGRAM 16. The double back somersault.

considered the extreme limits of twisting and somersaulting backwards.

The Press Handstand

The trick most commonly used to fulfill the strength requirement is a *press handstand* (Diagram 18). Strength is demonstrated by *pressing* (raising) the legs slowly off the floor up to a handstand position. This motion of rising slowly requires a great deal of back and shoulder strength. During the execution of the press, keep your arms and legs straight and, during the initial phase, lift your hips well above your head. Bending your arms or legs is poor technique. The ability to raise the hips well above the head comes from good flexibility. The pressing up of the legs should be slow, smooth, and continuous; pressing in a quick, jerky fashion is incorrect. Once in a handstand, hold

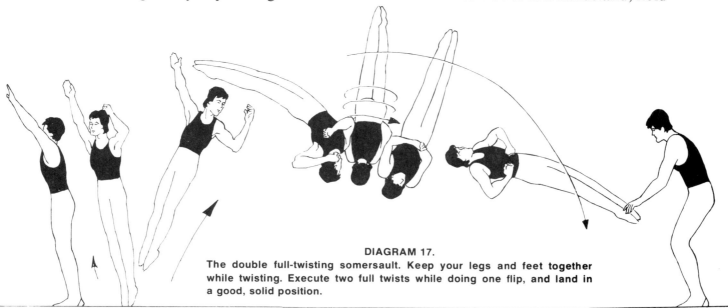

DIAGRAM 17.
The double full-twisting somersault. Keep your legs and feet together while twisting. Execute two full twists while doing one flip, and land in a good, solid position.

DIAGRAM 18. The press handstand.

the position securely for two full seconds.

POMMEL HORSE

The pommel horse is generally regarded as the most difficult gymnastics event for men. Many all-around championships have been won or lost on this event. In the United States collegiate meets, the pommel horse event is often won by a specialist.

To do well on the pommel horse, a man must have good balance and control. The event tends to suit tall gymnasts. As in floor exercise, smoothness of movement is an important factor in performing on the pommel horse.

Evaluation

Performers must fulfill the 11-part requirements I mentioned earlier. Other factors in evaluation of a routine are how often a gymnast turns to face a different direction and the number of times he travels to each section of the horse. If a gymnast touches the horse body with his feet, even slightly, his score is reduced. As a general rule, the man that continues to move without interruption will be rated the best performer.

A gymnast must perform part of his routine on each of the three sections of the horse. As the performer moves his body around the horse, he changes the position of his hands. Watching a gymnast's hands is often a good way for a spectator to recognize the difficulty of a move.

As in the other gymnastics events, there are an almost infinite number of movements possible on the pommel horse. Some of these variations are so quick and complicated that even experienced judges have been known to miss important parts. If you are a spectator, it is not important that you be able to recognize every specific routine. But you should be familiar with the major kinds of movements on the horse.

Starting Your Routine

You may begin your routine at either end of the horse or in the middle using both pommels.

Scissors

Scissors movements are performed by swinging back and forth in a scissorlike manner. To maintain proper balance, hold yourself high and lean well forward. A scis-

SCISSORS . . . must be lifted as high as possible. Big Eight champion Ralph Hernandez illustrates the hip height that is necessary to avoid deductions.

soring action of the legs should be executed as high as possible. Minimum standards specify that your hips should be lifted to shoulder height and your legs carried to a position well above your head. Even when your legs are apart, keep them straight and keep your feet pointed.

In your routine, you are required to use both *front scissors* (Diagram 19) and *reverse scissors* (Diagram 20).

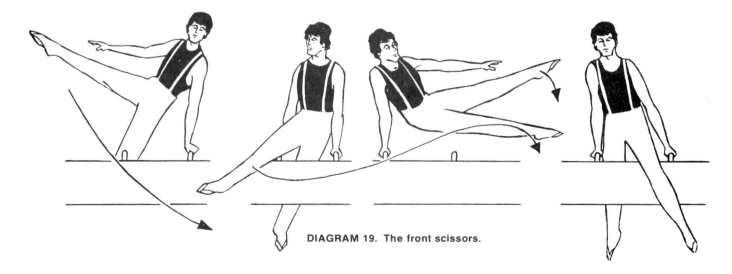

DIAGRAM 19. The front scissors.

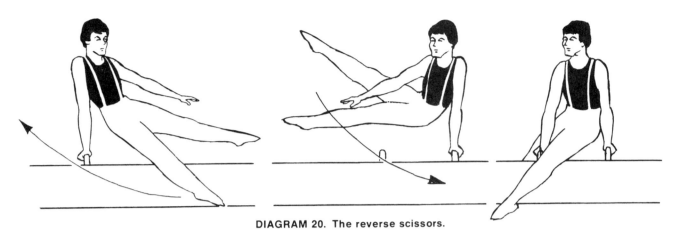

DIAGRAM 20. The reverse scissors.

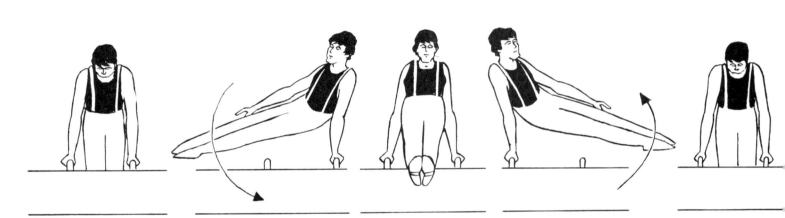

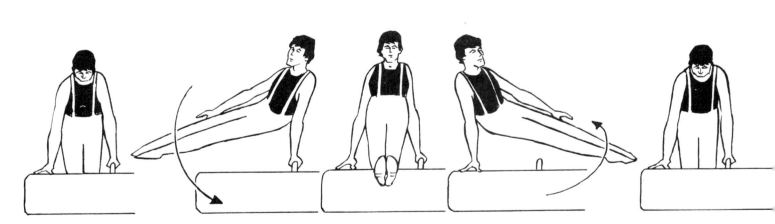

DIAGRAM 21.
Double leg circles. Your legs and body, from your shoulders down, must keep circling the horse at a constant, rapid speed. If you are forced to slow down because you lose your balance, you might hit the horse body with your feet or even fall off the horse. Keep your arms straight, lean well forward, and hold both legs and feet firmly together.

Another requirement for *leg work,* as scissors are commonly called, is that you must execute one of these scissors to both the right and the left. Scissors are rated as tricks of lower difficulty.

Since the front and reverse scissors are performed one after the other, introducing them in a performance provides a rather obvious change in tempo from the swinging action of the circles.

Circles

Before and after your leg work, you will perform variations of *double-leg circles* (Diagram 21). Like scissors, circles are tricks of lower difficulty. But, although they are relatively easy, you must perform them with careful attention to proper technique in order to avoid repeated deductions.

One of the crucial times during your horse routine is when you break out of circles into your leg work. This is very difficult to accomplish smoothly without touching the horse with at least one leg. This is where good balance and control become extremely important.

Intermediate and Superior Tricks

Scissors and circles fulfill the difficulty requirement for the five parts of lower value. The intermediate and superior requirements can be fulfilled in various ways. Often a new movement is invented by putting together the first half of one trick with the last half of another. Almost all intermediate movements are complicated variations of circles.

One exception is the *half-twisting front scissor* (Diagram 22). Adding this half-

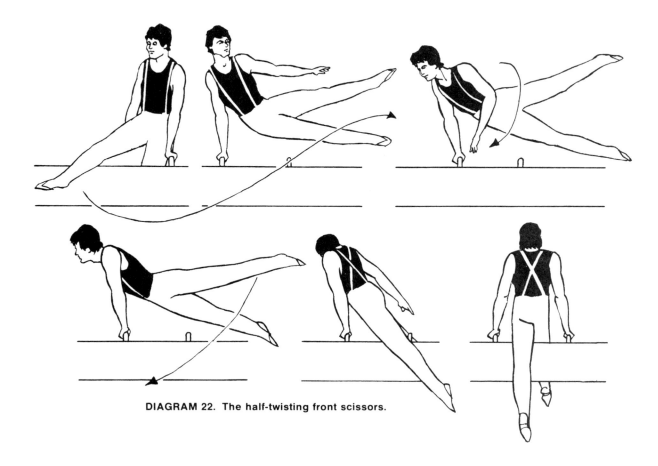

DIAGRAM 22. The half-twisting front scissors.

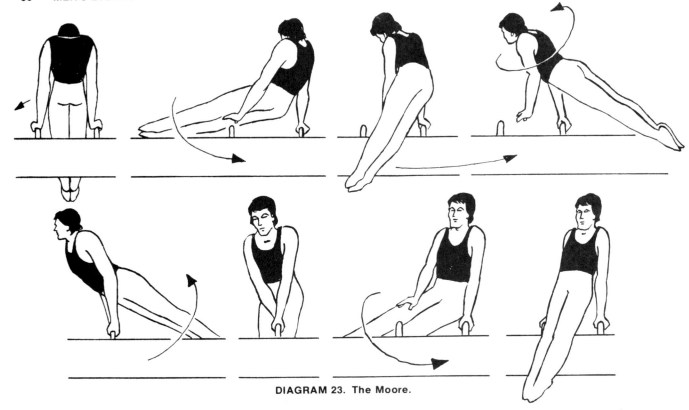

DIAGRAM 23. The Moore.

twist to the scissors movement increases it to the intermediate level.

A very common intermediate movement is the *Moore* (Diagram 23). While performing circles on the pommels, bring your hands together suddenly on one pommel, allowing your body to turn 180 degrees. Facing the new direction on the pommels, continue making circles.

Moving from one end of the horse up to

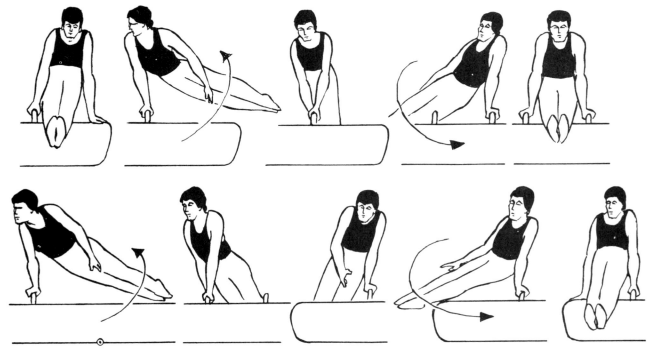

DIAGRAM 24. Travels.

the pommels and immediately down to the other end constitutes an intermediate part called *travels* (Diagram 24).

Another intermediate move is the *Stockli* (Diagram 25). While performing circles, move from the pommels to the end of the horse and then back onto the pommels.

Continue to invent variations, using these common tricks as examples. There are hundreds of combinations.

RINGS

To work rings effectively, you must develop strong arm and shoulder muscles. A gymnast working the rings usually has a well-developed upper torso.

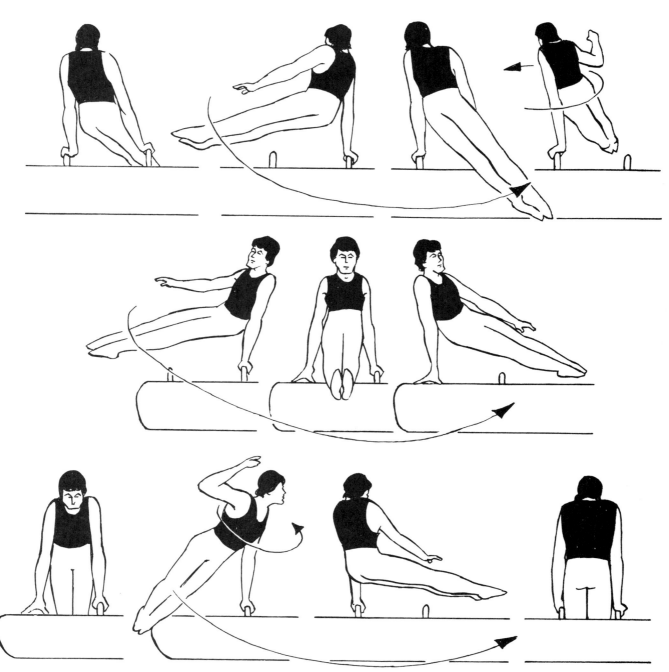

DIAGRAM 25. The Stockli.

Two major types of movements are performed on rings: *swinging parts* and *hold positions*. The term *swinging part* refers to a swinging action of the body, not of the rings. It is crucial that the rings remain as still as possible during the entire routine.

The swinging action around the rings is attained by a smooth, extended motion of the body. Good shoulder flexibility is very important, as is the ability to maintain a firm grip on the rings. Supporting the entire body weight through an 11-part routine requires handguards and well-callused hands.

Hold positions are usually motionless and require the gymnast to exhibit a great deal of upper-body strength. While executing a hold part, a gymnast must stop and show control in the hold position for a minimum of two full seconds. Failure to do so results in loss of value for the entire trick. As a rule, most routines will be designed with fewer hold positions than swinging parts.

Evaluation

Requirements for a routine on the rings include one hold position of intermediate difficulty and two handstands, one achieved with strength and one achieved by swinging from below the rings.

Any shaking of the rings or extra movement of the body will be seriously penalized. In satisfying the 11-part requirement on the rings, most gymnasts will demonstrate at least three handstands. In recent years, the *straight-arm technique* has added an extra element of virtuosity to the swinging parts. Although some gymnasts can execute an entire routine without once bending their arms, the introduction of just one movement using straight-arm work adds significantly to a gymnast's score.

Starting Your Routine

In mounting the equipment, you will usu-

ally be able to jump to a hanging position under your own power. However, since a routine should begin with complete stillness, it is sometimes necessary for your coach or a teammate to assist you to a still position. Most ringmen take this opportunity to obtain a secure grip.

Once your feet leave the ground, you are expected to hold good leg form. However, the routine begins officially only after you have been steadied and your assistant has stepped away. In some instances, a coach will remain under the rings in a spotting position. As long as the coach does not lend physical assistance, no points will be deducted. Verbal instructions are also prohibited. However, the mere presence of a spotter can be reassuring during a hazardous performance.

Hold Positions

A movement commonly used to fulfill the intermediate hold position requirement is the *iron cross* (Diagram 26). In the iron cross, the body is supported with the arms

DIAGRAM 26. The iron cross. Hold your arms straight and parallel to the floor. Bending your elbows or holding your shoulders too high above the rings will reduce your score, as will deviation from a vertical body position.

outstretched sideways. Showing strain in holding this position is considered poor technique.

The most frequently performed handstand with strength is a *hollow back press* (Diagram 27). While you perform this movement, your upward motion should be slow, smooth, and uninterrupted. The handstand position should be shown for two seconds.

DIAGRAM 27. The hollow-back press. Begin with a supported "L" position on top of the rings. Lower your legs slowly until your body is straight. Then, with your arms bent, lift your legs slowly into a handstand.

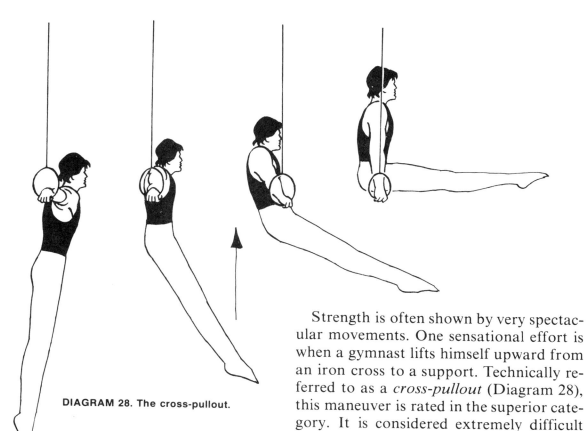

DIAGRAM 28. The cross-pullout.

Strength is often shown by very spectacular movements. One sensational effort is when a gymnast lifts himself upward from an iron cross to a support. Technically referred to as a *cross-pullout* (Diagram 28), this maneuver is rated in the superior category. It is considered extremely difficult just to hold the iron cross; adding a pullout action is a remarkable feat.

Equally recognized as a superior strength move is the *Maltese* (Diagram 29). In this position, you must hold your body in a horizontal support position above the rings. As in all hold parts on rings, this position must be shown for two seconds.

Both the cross-pullout and the Maltese are tricks of extreme skill. Very seldom will superior hold parts be used by the all-around man. Strength of this magnitude is generally developed only through specialization.

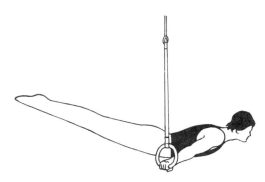

DIAGRAM 29. The Maltese.

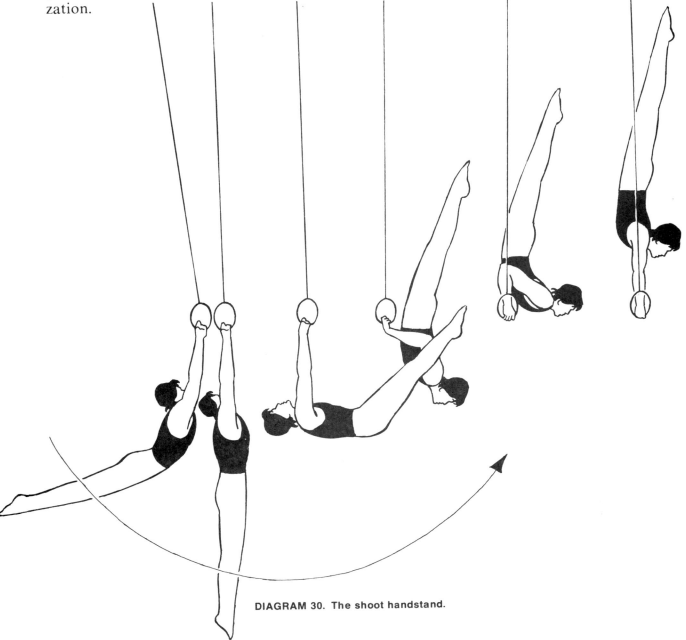

DIAGRAM 30. The shoot handstand.

Swinging Parts

The second handstand requirement is most often fulfilled by demonstrating a *shoot handstand* (Diagram 30). Swing your body forward around the rings and up to a handstand position. Most important here is the smooth, quick, and unhesitating swing of your body up the handstand. Any interruption prior to a balanced handstand is

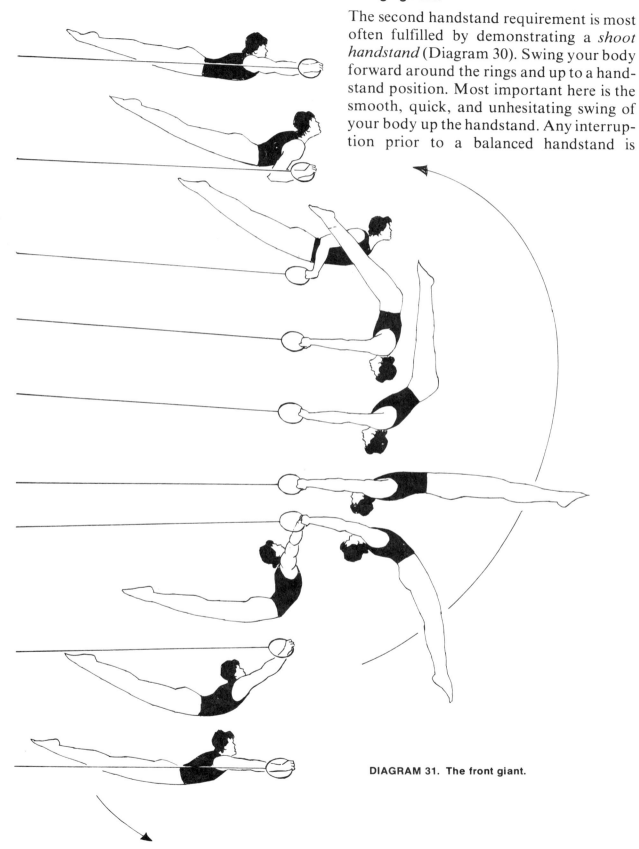

DIAGRAM 31. The front giant.

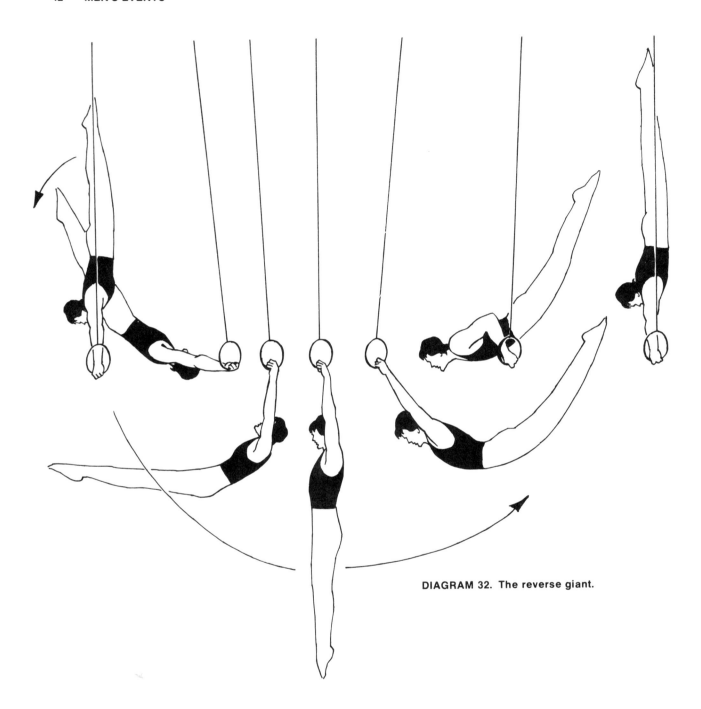

DIAGRAM 32. The reverse giant.

considered improper. Again, the handstand must be held firmly balanced for two seconds.

Movements that start from a handstand position and swing in a complete 360-degree circle back up to a handstand position are referred to as *giants*. They can be performed either as *front* (Diagram 31) or *reverse* giants (Diagram 32), depending on the direction of the swing. Giants are similar to the shoot handstand. The primary difference is that giants originate from above and the shoot handstand is initiated from below the rings.

DIAGRAM 33. The double back somersault.

DIAGRAM 34. The full-twisting somersault.

Dismounts

Rings *dismounts* are a good example of how a technique learned on the ground can be transferred to the air. What might be considered a simple feat to perform from a foot take off in floor exercise might be rated as twice as difficult when performed from a hand-release on rings.

Two of the most common rings dismounts are the *double back somersault* (Diagram 33) and the *full-twisting back somersault* (Diagram 34). Both dismounts are rated in the superior category. Two factors that are used to evaluate these dismounts are the height of the dismount above the rings and the degree of control on landing.

Recently it has been popular to attempt the double back somersault from the rings with the legs straight in a pike position. This is considered much more difficult than using the conventional tuck style position. Adding the piked element earns a gymnast more points for risk.

Another dismount of high risk is the double-twisting back somersault. Considered much more difficult to accomplish on rings than on floor exercise, it is classified as a superior part.

VAULTING

Vaulting is the only event in the all-around program that is not governed by the 11-part requirement. Instead, only one part is required—a single movement (vault) performed over the length of a horse body. Vaulting relies on strong leg muscles. A good vaulter must be able to run quickly and jump from the springboard aggressively.

Evaluation

Ninety percent of a vault's height and distance is created by a fast run coupled with the muscular lifting power of the legs. Even though the approach is not evaluated, a vaulter is limited to a maximum run of 20 meters. He may elect to start his approach anywhere within this maximum limit, but he must continue with his vault once he has taken the first step.

It is a technical requirement for a vaulter to push off the horse with his hands at some point during his flight. Touching the horse accidentally with the feet or any other part of the body, however, results in a severe deduction. International rules stipulate that the horse be divided and marked into two zones. A gymnast is expected to place his hands in only one zone. Touching the center dividing line in the middle of the horse results in a 0.50 points deduction.

In the evaluation of a vault, the flight over the horse is divided into two technical categories. The first is referred to as the *pre-flight* (Diagram 35). Specifically, pre-flight

20°

DIAGRAM 35. The pre-flight phase of the vault.

is judged according to the angle of a performer's body to the horse. At the precise moment a gymnast pushes off the horse with his hands, the angle or pre-flight must be a minimum of 20 degrees above the horizontal top surface of the horse.

The second category is the *post-flight*

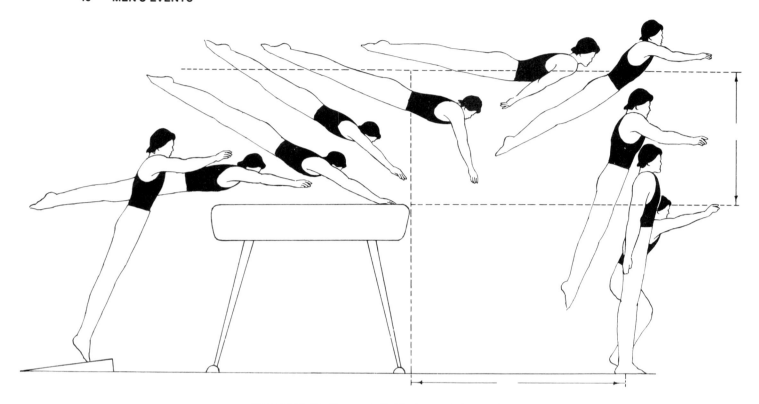

DIAGRAM 36. The post-flight phase of the vault.

(Diagram 36). The emphasis in post-flight is to establish height and distance above and beyond the far end of the horse. A gymnast is expected to demonstrate a direction of flight that increases in trajectory. The post-flight should be higher than the pre-flight. The body must rise in such a way that the buttocks are four-fifths of the height of the horse above the horse.

In one respect, vaulting is evaluated in much the same way as diving. According to the FIG (Federation of International Gymnastics) Code of Points, each vault is given a set maximum value based upon its degree of difficulty. Since only one vault is allowed, most collegiate competitors will select a trick rated as near as possible to a 10.0 (perfect score). Naturally a 10.0 is very seldom, if ever, attained; however, selecting a vault of high value will immediately prevent a point deduction for lack of difficulty.

Since a vaulting routine is made up of only one trick, each aspect of the vault must be critically evaluated. As a result, demonstrating a secure, well-controlled landing is of special importance. Proper landing stance allows for a reasonable bend of the hips and knees. However, even if the gymnast is not forced to take an extra step, squatting too low or bending the upper body forward below the horizontal level is considered poor landing posture. After a reasonable flexing of the hips and legs, the body should be perfectly erect. In addition, appropriate deductions are given for failing to land at a minimum distance beyond the end of the horse.

To provide a foundation for more accurate evaluation, vaulting rules for finals are more demanding than regulations used in preliminaries. In preliminaries for larger competitions or for dual meets, the vaulter is allowed to have only one vault evaluated.

In large open championships, conference championships, NCAA championships, and the Olympic Games, a final session is held for the top finalists in each event. In this final round, the vaulters are required to perform two different vaults; the scores of both vaults are then averaged.

Starting Your Vault

From an erect standing position, run down the runway, increasing your momentum with each stride. Spring off the board at the moment of maximum acceleration.

Vaulting Movements

In past years the *Yamashita* (Diagram 37) has proved to be one of the most popular vaults. It was named after a Japanese gymnast who was the first to perform the movement in competition.

To correctly execute a full-twisting handspring (Diagram 38), a gymnast must pay particular attention to proper form. Keep your legs straight and hold them firmly together; this proper leg form is especially difficult to demonstrate on this particular trick. Make certain that you achieve the complete full twist, not just ⅛ of it. Being shy of completing the twist is a common error.

Not as commonly used as the full-twisting handspring but more spectacular is the double front somersault (Diagram 39). This vault has a high risk factor because you must turn (flip) two complete times before landing. As a rule, the critical point in the evaluation will be whether you can land in a proper standing position. Hitting the mat while still in the tuck position, or having to make several quick steps to attain balance, is considered weak technique. In spite of the extreme difficulty of this trick you are still expected to show complete control.

DIAGRAM 37. The Yamashita.

DIAGRAM 38. The full-twisting handspring.

DIAGRAM 39. The double front somersault.

DIAGRAM 40. The cartwheel back somersault.

In recent years a new 10.0 vault, the *cartwheel back somersault* (Diagram 40), has presented a real challenge for the advanced vaulter. It is actually a combination of several different vaults. To do this vault correctly, make a special effort to keep your legs together and to maintain your balance on landing. The somersault may be performed as a tuck or a pike. A pike position (legs straight) is more points for risk.

PARALLEL BARS

Nearly every conceivable gymnastics trick is adaptable to the parallel bars. The design of the bars makes it possible for the gym-

**DIAGRAM 41.
The basic handstand position on the parallel bars.**

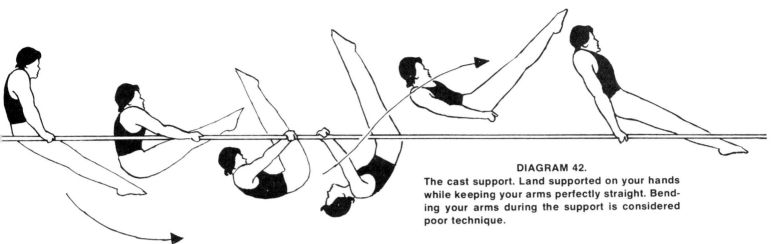

DIAGRAM 42.
The cast support. Land supported on your hands while keeping your arms perfectly straight. Bending your arms during the support is considered poor technique.

nast to duplicate many skills performed in the other five all-around events. For example, a gymnast can perform pommel horse circles and even some of the strength parts that are normally seen on rings. Somersaults that are used on floor exercise and vaulting are also used on the bars. At times, a gymnast will also work sideways on one rail to demonstrate a skill similar to those used on the high bar.

Another distinguishing characteristic of the parallel bars is that the gymnast must release one or both hands during virtually every movement. Releasing and regripping the bars repeatedly subjects the gymnast to numerous opportunities for error. Because excelling under these conditions requires great versatility, in most cases, the parallel bars prove to be an all-around man's strongest event.

A generous application of chalk, along with the added protection of handguards, is a necessity. As on the rings, the gymnast who works parallel bars must develop a good set of callused hands in order to avoid painful rips.

To demonstrate appropriate technique on the parallel bars, a gymnast must have proper extended body position and shoulder flexibility. Correct extension is illustrated by the basic handstand position (Diagram 41). Avoid showing a curved posture or an arched position in your back. Keep your body straight and elongated. This is not only more esthetic but it proves to be a technical asset for your performance. If you work with an arched body position, you will look heavy and tend to tire quickly. Performing with an extended body position allows you to swing in a manner that takes less energy and looks more appealing.

DIAGRAM 43. The cut-catch to L-hold.

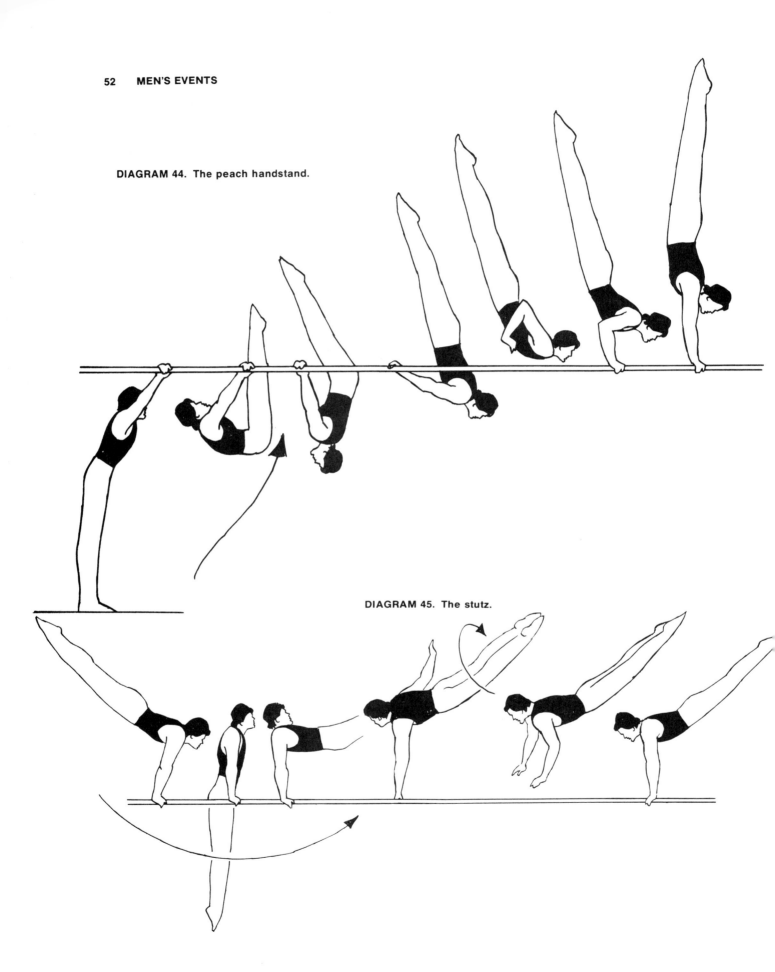

DIAGRAM 44. The peach handstand.

DIAGRAM 45. The stutz.

Evaluation

A routine is expected to flow smoothly; a gymnast is allowed only three stop positions. Using more than three stops results in a penalty. A pause of two full seconds is considered a stop position on parallel bars. A move held longer than three seconds is improper.

In completing the 11-part requirement, a gymnast is expected to demonstrate at least one movement of intermediate difficulty both above and below the bars. Both of these intermediate moves must be performed from a simultaneous two-handed release.

The gymnast's greatest concern is designing a routine with full difficulty. Normally the five parts of low difficulty that are required would be easily fulfilled; however, on the parallel bars, even this category becomes difficult to satisfy when arranging a routine.

A movement on parallel bars is classified either as a *swinging part* or a *strength part*, the same classification that is used on rings. An additional requirement is that the superior trick be a swinging part. Fortunately, this rule is easily fulfilled, since most superior parts on the parallel bars are swinging parts.

Mounts

You are allowed to mount the equipment from within the bars, from either end, or from the side. A springboard, the type used for vaulting, is also available for your use if you should so desire. The purpose of a springboard, in this case, is to provide you an opportunity to demonstrate a mount that requires a running approach. Almost any movement performed as a mount can also be executed as a part in the middle of a routine.

One of the most common starts is a *cast support* (Diagram 42). A cast support receives an intermediate rating; however, if

FORM . . . is carefully evaluated by the judges. Here Big Eight Conference all-around champion Jim Stephenson demonstrates correct foot, leg, arm, and body form for the hecht dismount.

followed with a *cut-catch to L-hold* (Diagram 43) the entire sequence is rated superior in value. Therefore this combination is frequently used to satisfy the superior requirement.

Another mount used quite often is the *peach handstand* (Diagram 44). It receives a superior rating as a single part. One special stipulation is that the final position of this movement must terminate in a handstand position held for two seconds. Should you fail to fulfill this minimum time requirement, the peach handstand is reduced to intermediate value.

Parallel Bars Movements

One of the most desirable and necessary parts of a championship performance is the *stutz* (Diagram 45), which is used primarily as a movement to change direction. The

DIAGRAM 46. The stutz, superior rating.

value of the stutz depends on the height established during the turn. To be given a low difficulty rating, the turn must be at least horizontal with the bars. When the turn occurs at least 30 degrees above the horizontal, it is rated as intermediate. In order to be classified as superior, the stutz must turn and terminate in a handstand position (Diagram 46) held for two seconds. If the handstand is held for less than two seconds, the stutz is reduced to intermediate value. Although most gymnasts are content with meeting the minimum requirements to earn the intermediate rating, executing this movement at the superior level is a characteristic of a true champion.

The stutz handstand has led to the development of a new movement, the *Diamidov*.

DIAGRAM 47. The Diamidov.

Named after the Russian gymnast who first performed this move in international competition, a Diamidov is basically a full spin turn on one arm (Diagram 47). The movement begins like the stutz. The main difference occurs at the release point. In the Diamidov, only one hand is released, allowing the body to pivot one full spin around one supporting arm. The Diamidov need not terminate in a handstand position to receive full difficulty. However, attaining the handstand position for at least one-half second is most desirable in illustrating proper technique.

DIAGRAM 48. The front somersault.

Dismounts

The parallel bars provide opportunities to execute a wide variety of dismounts. Two of the most popular are the *front* and *back somersaults* (Diagrams 48 and 49). Both are rated as movements of lesser difficulty. You can increase them to intermediate moves by incorporating a half-twist.

Considered to be extremely difficult moves of superior rating, are the *full-twisting back somersault* (Diagram 50) and the *double back somersault* (Diagram 51).

DIAGRAM 49. The back somersault.

DIAGRAM 50. The full-twisting back somersault.

DIAGRAM 51. The double back somersault.

HORIZONTAL BAR (HIGH BAR)

The high bar, the last event in a gymnastics meet, is considered the most spectacular. This distinction is deserved because of the sensationally high dismounts that end each routine.

Equally amazing is the degree of stress put on the arms and shoulders, and especially the hands. Chalk and handguards are an obvious necessity, but even more important to the gymnast is the development of strong, well-callused palms. Of the six events, the high bar is the hardest on the hands. The only way to avoid rips is to start out slowly, remembering not to overwork at any one time, and to keep a consistent workout schedule. In spite of the fact that high bar is rough on the hands, an experienced competitor is able to avoid rips almost entirely by using a well-organized workout program.

A noticeable buildup of chalk remains coated on the bar after each routine. Normally this causes little difficulty; however, after a few routines it may be necessary to remove some of the chalk with an emery cloth in order to assure a firm grip. Be careful not to remove every bit of chalk, however, since a perfectly clear bar tends to feel slippery.

Evaluation

Like other events, the high bar has an 11-part requirement. An almost endless variety of complicated moves may be used to satisfy these requirements. Most of the

moves are similar to those performed on the parallel bars and in other events.

The position of the hands is a key point of reference, since a routine on the high bar is primarily composed of variations in grip changes during the execution of giant swings. The gymnast must strive for a smooth, continuous motion without stops. Hesitations, or hold positions, are considered poor technique.

In addition to the grip placement of the hands, the judges watch for additional variations in movements. These can be created by swinging or holding the body in a pike position near the bar instead of holding the body stretched out away from the bar. In either case, it is necessary to have a proper grip to match the direction of swing.

I won't attempt to illustrate all the complicated giant swings or combinations. Instead I will talk about only the basic movements. An endless variety of hand placements can result in an equal variety of movements. Basically, any change in hand placement combined with a turning action of the body during a giant swing will create a movement of intermediate or superior difficulty.

Mounts

When approaching the bar, you may mount from either direction. As you jump from the floor to a hanging position on the bar, establish a small initial pendulum swing to gain a slight advantage in performing the first movement. Although this small preliminary swing is not recognized as a trick, it is considered necessary and will not result in a penalty, as long as you do not take more than one swing back and forth.

Since most high bar routines begin with the same movement, the *stemme,* it is an excellent starting point for examining the more common elements of high bar. A stemme (Diagram 52) is easily performed from the initial pendulum swing, and it is by far the quickest way to attain an ex-

tended handstand position above the bar. (The handstand position is not held). From this advantage point, you can begin your first giant swing from your highest position. Difficulty rating for the stemme is based upon its nearness to a vertical handstand position. Anything within five degrees of being vertical is considered sufficient. A stemme executed at a lower angle has no value, but no additional deduction for poor execution is imposed.

DIAGRAM 52. The stemme.

Movements on the High Bar

The basic swings around the bar are the *giants*, which are similar to giants performed on rings. On the high bar, however, you must switch the position of your hands when you change direction of swing.

As you swing your body forward when executing front giants, use a front overhand grip. When you swing backwards through reverse giants, use a reverse (under) grip. There can be no exceptions. Failing to use the proper grip in either direction will cause you to release your hold as you pass through the bottom point of your swing.

The front and reverse *stalders* (Diagrams 53 and 54) are directly related to the front and reverse giants. Rated as superior parts, both are characterized by a straddling action of the legs past the bar. Give careful observance to your legs and arms. Keep your elbows straight and locked and avoid bending your knees or scraping your feet against the bar. Stalders should also terminate in a near handstand position. Any significant deviation from this vertical completion point is considered poor technique.

In satisfying the combination requirement of showing a dorsal hang or grip, most gymnasts will execute a *stoop through* from reverse giants (Diagram 55). Pay particular attention to keeping your legs perfectly straight when you pull your feet in between your hands over the bar. Bending the knees even slightly is considered a form break. Requiring a high degree of flexibility, this movement can be considerably difficult to perform. An interruption, such as hitting the feet on the bar, is a common occurrence.

One additional requirement calls for a trick showing a simultaneous release of both grips, followed by regrasping the bar with both hands simultaneously. One of the most obvious movements showing this essential element is the *vault*, a move of intermediate rating (Diagram 56). The main distinguishing feature of the vault is that when you release both hands you allow the body to sail in a free-floating manner over the bar. You then regrasp with both hands simultaneously on the other side of the bar. The simultaneous releasing and regrasping is the critical feature. However, height and sureness of execution are also important.

Dismounts

Dismounts from the high bar are nothing short of sensational. The average height of most dismounts is well over 12 feet in the air. This tremendous elevation is a result of the high rate of centrifugal force developed at the end of each giant swing.

Dismounts used by collegiate competitors vary from single somersaults of lesser value to multiple flips with twists (Diagram 57), which are rated in the superior category. The critical factor in being able to accomplish the more complicated dismounts is the ability to gain sufficient height. This can be a problem for the man who runs out of energy or is a little reluctant to release the bar properly. A slight misjudgment in timing can cause a dismount to overturn or be short of the proper landing point. Being able to show a controlled finish is of special importance. It can be an extremely frustrating situation for a competitor to execute a flawless routine, only to complete his dismount in an awkward position.

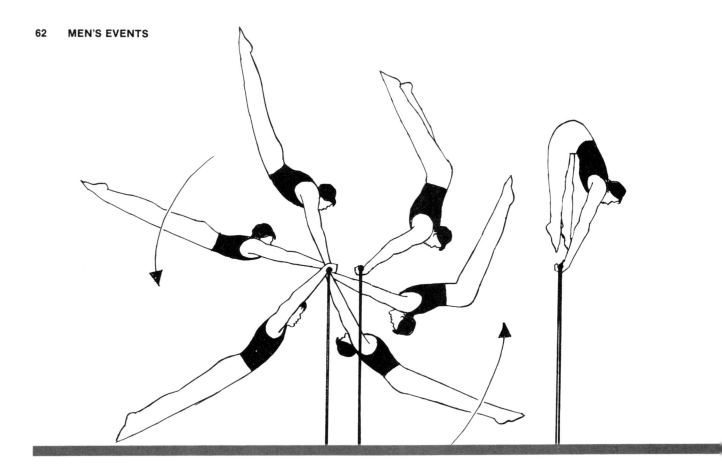

DIAGRAM 54. The reverse stalder.

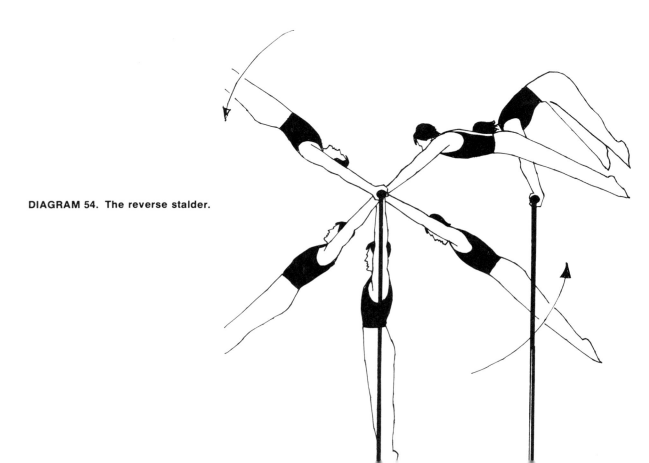

DIAGRAM 53. The front stalder.

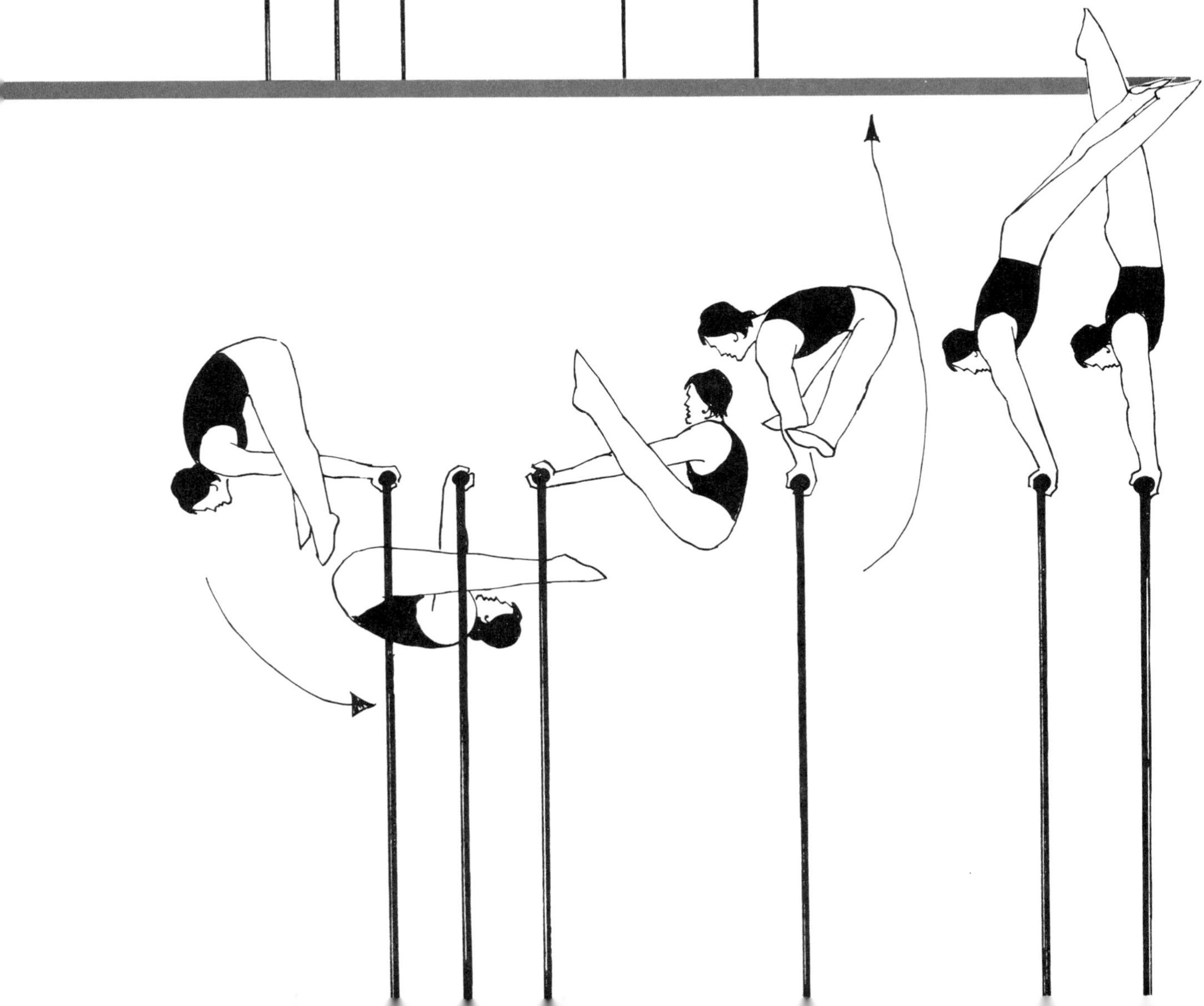

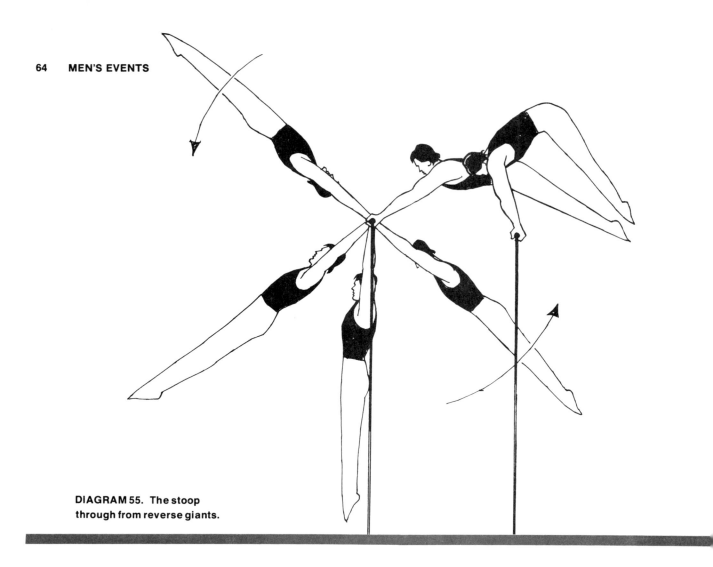

**DIAGRAM 55. The stoop
through from reverse giants.**

DIAGRAM 56. The vault.

DIAGRAM 57.   Multiple-flip dismounts from the high bar.

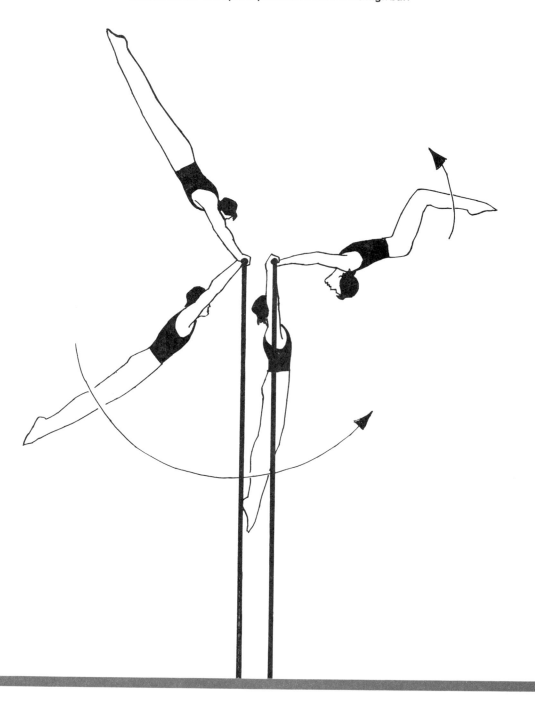

THE LUNGE POSE . . . is one of the numerous pose movements that can be incorporated into a routine on the balance beam.

chapter 5
WOMEN'S EVENTS

Each of the four events in women's gymnastics has a specific purpose, and each uses equipment suited to a woman's body structure. Although each women's event demands a high degree of muscular development, suppleness and flexibility are equally necessary. By participating in all four events, a gymnast develops excellent posture and muscular control.

As in men's gymnastics, important movements will often be transferred from event to event. For example, it is quite common for a floor exercise trick to be used on the balance beam as well.

International rules allow only a female coach to be on the floor of competition. In the United States, men as well as women are allowed to coach. Even internationally, where men are not allowed on the floor of competition, they often assist behind the scenes during practice sessions. One coaching situation that works very well is having a male coach teach the more risky tumbling movements that require spotting

and a woman coach teach the dance and organizational features of a routine.

The women's total program requires compulsories as well as optionals. Performing a portion of the compulsory as an optional sequence is considered improper and results in a deduction. A compulsory movement is permissible only when it has a different preceding or succeeding part.

FLOOR EXERCISE

Like the similar men's event, women's floor exercise is based primarily on tumbling movements. However, because women's gymnastics emphasizes grace and flexibility more than strength, women's floor exercise uses smoother, dancelike movements in the transitional sequences.

Women are not expected to hold balance positions any longer than is necessary to show control. In fact, a movement held too long is penalized because the gymnast has broken the continuity of her routine.

Because it consists of dance movements, women's floor exercise is accompanied by music. Each gymnast provides her own accompaniment, suited to her style. The music can be live or taped.

Live music, usually on the piano, has some advantages over taped music. The main advantage is in timing. With live accompaniment, the music can be kept in tempo with the movements of the gymnast. Unintentional hesitations by the performer can be compensated for by the musician, keeping the gymnast's performance in proper harmony with the music. Live music is common for international or Olympic competitions.

Taped music sets a rigid tempo for the gymnast to follow. Normally, two or three different musical numbers will be spliced together to complement slow-, medium-, and fast-moving sequences. Once put together, these edited musical selections somewhat limit a performer who wants to design a new routine. Even a slight deviation, such as the addition of a new part or sequence, requires an appropriate adjustment in the musical arrangement. As a result, the continual process of rearranging music can be as difficult a task as developing a routine.

Evaluation

Competitive floor exercises must last from one minute to one minute and 30 seconds. Since most routines are performed to music on pretimed tapes, the gymnast will pay little or no attention to the official timer. However, should the time limit be violated, an exercise that is too short is penalized 0.05 point for each second under one minute. An exercise lasting over the legal limit is penalized 0.3 point. The judges end their evaluation at the maximum time limit.

Upon receiving a signal from the head judge, a gymnast walks over and assumes a starting position on the floor exercise mat. A routine is usually preceded by a short musical introduction; however, evaluation does not begin until the gymnast's first movement. If, at the beginning of an exercise, a gymnast stops herself and begins again due to her personal fault, a penalty is assessed. However, is she stops as a result of technical difficulties encountered with the music, a second trial will be allowed without penalty.

DIAGRAM 58. The aerial walkover.

In moving from one sequence to another, the gymnast must make effective use of the entire area. A floor pattern that uses curvilinear as well as straight paths should be used in moving to all parts of the mat.

Turns should be executed at different points around the area, not just in the corners. A gymnast should not remain in one spot too long or return to one section repeatedly and exclude parts of the remaining floor area.

Throughout her performance, the gymnast is expected to demonstrate a varied arrangement of sequences that express suppleness, grace, and dynamism, without loss of body control. Other skills a gymnast's routine should demonstrate include:

1. Good balance, showing a firm and steady body.
2. Coordination of the arms and legs with the upper trunk to express proper stretch and carriage of the upper body.
3. Execution of dynamic tumbles, pivots, leaps, and jumps, while still maintaining proper lightness on landings.
4. Good flexibility and suppleness in coordinating all parts of the body.

A routine of full difficulty must be composed of four average and three superior movements. Nearly all superior movements will be in the tumbling category. The dance category, which includes such movements as leaps, pivots, turns, and jumps, is usually composed of movements of medium difficulty. One exception is the *full turn or pivot ending in a balance*, a dance movement that is rated superior.

Floor Exercise Movements

The *aerial walkover* is an extremely popular superior movement that requires the high degree of flexibility naturally displayed by women gymnasts (Diagram 58). Begin the aerial walkover with an explosive lift from the floor. The elevation of your walkover should be above your shoulder height, and your landing must be soft. Bending either leg while you turn over or land is considered poor execution.

Since tumbling is such an important feature of floor exercise, high somersaulting maneuvers are important. One such maneuver, which can be executed with great height, is the *layout back somersault* (Diagram 59). The height of the somersault should be above your head. During a back layout, your body should be in a straight or slightly arched position, and your legs should be extended. A common variation that you can use when landing is to spread your legs and land on one foot. The one-foot landing is more appealing if you spread your legs as far apart as possible. Whatever landing you use, avoid landing with an abrupt stop.

As a rule, women's backward tumbling is usually limited to a layout back somersault, except at the Olympic level, where competitors often go a step further by adding a full twist. And, on a few occasions, gymnasts have been known to execute the difficult double-twisting back somersault.

Two of the most widely used movements

DIAGRAM 59. The layout back somersault.

of medium difficulty are the *front* and *back walkovers*. Both of these movements (Diagrams 60 & 61) require flexibility in the upper and lower back. To execute these movements, split your legs completely while you are upside down. Failing to do a complete split, bending your legs, or landing in a heavy, jerky fashion are all considered unattractive. It is important that both front and back walkovers be executed with complete control and smoothness.

In combining the more difficult tumbling elements with the transitional dance parts, use only those sequences suited to your

DIAGRAM 60. The front walkover.

DIAGRAM 61. The back walkover.

ability. Have confidence in yourself—only then will you be able to express lively and exciting maneuvers in perfect harmony with the music.

BALANCE BEAM

A good gymnast performs on the balance beam with such ease and grace that it looks deceptively simple. In reality, however, mastering the balance beam requires precise balance and control.

Elements of difficulty must be evenly distributed throughout the composition, and the gymnast must make use of the entire beam length.

In addition to the above, a properly de-

signed balance beam routine should contain the following elements:

1. Movements executed in both upright and inverted positions.
2. Turns on one foot in both the left and right directions that go beyond 180 degrees.
3. Leaps and jumps with vertical height and horizontal distances.
4. A variety of stepping movements that includes large and small running steps in combination with appropriate arm and leg configurations.
5. An assortment of positions, including crouching, sitting, or lying on the beam. However, the routine should be dominated by the standing movements.

A gymnast must design her routine to last from 1 minute and 15 seconds to 1 minute and 35 seconds. Timing begins as soon as the gymnast's feet leave the floor or the board and ends at the moment a gymnast's feet make contact with the mats on the dismount. A warning signal is given at 1 minute, 30 seconds and 1 minute, 35 seconds.

Mounts

To begin your routine, you have the option of using a springboard to provide extra explosive power on takeoff. The springboard allows you to perform more complicated, versatile mounts. A board can be placed in any desirable location. Normally, it is removed by your coach once you have mounted the beam, to eliminate the possibility of your accidentally falling on the board if you lose your balance on the beam.

You are allowed to mount the beam from any desirable angle. An important consideration here, as with the dismount, is that the mount should correspond in difficulty to the internal structure of the routine. In other words, if you are demonstrating a routine of advanced skill, you should execute a mount and dismount of advanced difficulty.

Evaluation

Many movements on the balance beam are the same as those performed in floor exercise. However, because of the greater degree of risk, the same movements often receive a higher rating on the beam than on the floor. For example, dance parts made up of pivots and leaps are usually classified as medium parts on floor exercise; they are in many instances considered superior movements on the beam.

From the first moment the gymnast touches the beam, she must continue her routine without hesitating. If a gymnast falls to the floor during a routine, she must remount the beam within 10 seconds. A fall results in a 0.50 points penalty. During this period the clock is kept running. Should a performance run overtime, the gymnast is penalized 0.3 points. In addition, the judges discontinue their evaluation at this point. In some cases this could mean losing value for the dismount and being penalized for performing a routine without a dismount. An exercise that is too short is penalized 0.05 points for each second under the time.

An important consideration with regard to falls is whether or not credit is given for the trick causing the fall. If the gymnast almost completes the trick before she falls, she will still receive credit for the movement. However, if the fall occurs in the middle of the movement, no credit is awarded.

In general, body carriage and good posture are of utmost importance. Keeping a balance between dance and tumbling movements should also be a basic objective. Neither category must predominate.

In addition to the basic requirements of three superior and four average skills, a routine must contain certain additional elements. Balance is extremely critical, as is maintaining well-controlled body movements while still demonstrating freedom and ease of execution.

The rhythm of a performance should be smooth and uninterrupted. Following the new international concept of *continuous beam movement*, a gymnast should demonstrate continuous execution, uninterrupted except for a maximum of three *stops* (still positions). A great number of stops must be penalized, even if the gymnast tries to cover up these rest periods by visible movements with the arms. A slow exercise with pauses to attain stability lessens the value of the exercise.

One of the most popular mounts is the *press handstand mount* (Diagram 62), which is often used as a superior part. You may execute this mount on either the end or the side of the beam. Two basic variations are possible: you may keep your legs together or spread them apart in a straddled position. In either case, the value remains the same. Check to see that you keep your arms and legs straight. Your upward movement should be smooth and continuous and terminate in a well-stretched handstand. Avoid jerky or labored movements.

You may also do a press handstand in the middle of your routine, starting from a standing position on the beam. Since this is not as difficult as starting the handstand

DIAGRAM 62. The press handstand mount.

from the ground, it is reduced to a medium rating.

Another impressive mount is the *forward walkover* (Diagram 63). This maneuver requires a running approach combined with a take off from the springboard. Bending the arms or failing to maintain continuous motion while turning over is considered improper. Rated as superior, this mount is generally recognized as being one of the most difficult to perform.

Movements on the Beam

When executing pivots or turns, demonstrate correct body alignment (good stretch) and a continuous, well-balanced

DIAGRAM 63. The forward walkover.

DIAGRAM 64. The stag leap.

position on the balls of your feet. Usually, there should be no dropping of your heel before you complete your turn.

One of the most recognizable leaps is the *stag leap* (Diagram 64). As in many gymnastics movements, it is desirable to demonstrate height in performing this maneuver. You need *amplitude*, the maximum possible lift or extension of the legs, in moving your body through an upward outward direction. Kick your legs to as wide a *split* as possible. Execute leaps such as the stag with a dynamic takeoff initiated with the legs and feet. Your landing should appear light and effortless.

Tumbling movements are among the most spectacular features of a performance on the balance beam. Advanced competitors almost always use a cartwheel (medium part). If you perform this same cartwheel with one arm instead of two arms, it is raised to a superior part. To execute the cartwheel properly (Diagram 65), face sideward while turning over. Move your legs in a plane directly over the beam and spread them as wide as possible. Avoid hesitation. A smooth action showing a 1-2-3-4 rhythmical contact of hand, hand, foot, foot, is technically correct.

In the *front* and *back walkovers* (Dia-

DIAGRAM 65. The cartwheel.

grams 66 and 67), difficulty again depends on whether one or two arms are used. If you use two arms to support your body, the walkover is given medium value; if you use only one arm, it is awarded superior value.

Dismounts

To complete your routine, you may choose from a variety of front or back somersaults, with or without twists, that can be executed to the side or off the end of the beam. One of the most common superior dismounts is the *Barani* (Diagram 68). Basically a layout front somersault with a half twist, it is evaluated on height obtained and the degree of body extension in flight. As is true for dismounts on all events, height is of critical importance. Any somersault executed with a twist is considered more difficult than a dismount with no twist.

UNEVEN PARALLEL BARS (BARS)

Hanging and supporting positions on the bars demand proper development of muscles in the shoulders, arms, and abdomen. Unlike the other three women's events, bars primarily require upper torso strength. Although strength is necessary, the movements performed on bars should not be slow, static muscular actions. Strength

DIAGRAM 66. The one-arm front walkover.

DIAGRAM 67. The one-arm back walkover.

DIAGRAM 68. The Barani, basically a layout front somersault with a half-twist.

should be hidden in a free flow of swinging movements.

Evaluation

Current gymnastics emphasizes continuous swinging throughout a bars routine, avoiding stops as much as possible. When the nature of a movement demands a pause, it should be as short as possible. Any still position is considered a rest point and is penalized accordingly.

A routine should consist primarily of swinging movements circling around the bars, with *kipping* moves that demonstrate releases and regrasps from one bar to another. All tricks, including changes in direction, should be executed with uninterrupted motion and good form.

UPPER BAR MOVEMENTS . . . should be as
predominant as those on the lower bar.

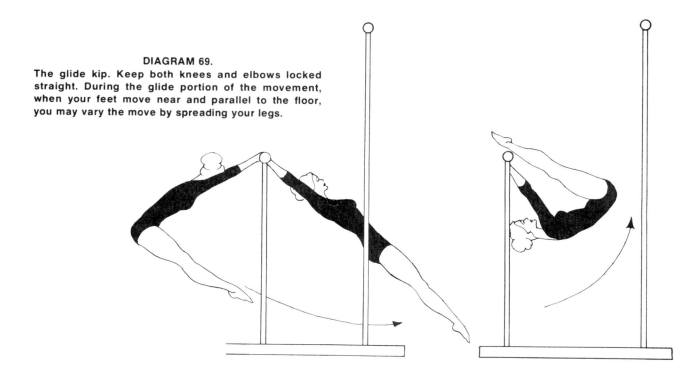

DIAGRAM 69.
The glide kip. Keep both knees and elbows locked straight. During the glide portion of the movement, when your feet move near and parallel to the floor, you may vary the move by spreading your legs.

Four average and three superior parts should be included in a routine, along with the necessary connecting transitions, for a total of 12 to 14 movements. The more difficult parts should be evenly distributed throughout the routine, and the gymnast should perform a mount and dismount that are equal in difficulty to the total routine. Emphasis should be placed upon graceful movements—men's strength positions are not acceptable.

If she falls, a gymnast is penalized 0.50 points. During a recovery period, 30 seconds is allowed for rechalking and readjusting of handguards. In continuing after a fall, a gymnast may not repeat any portion of the exercise she has already attempted. Failing to continue after 30 seconds terminates the exercise.

If you are performing on the bars, you must take especially good care of your hands, which will become sore and hot from swinging on the bars. Use chalk to provide a secure grip. Equally important to the advanced performer is a protective pair of handguards. The more chalk you use, the more often it will be necessary to remove excess chalk that accumulates on the rails. Emery cloth is used for this purpose. Some gymnasts prefer to apply chalk to the rails as well as to their hands. This keeps the bars uniformly dry and prevents running out of chalk midway through a routine.

Mounts

After you receive the starting signal from the judge, you may approach the bars from either side. As in the balance beam event, you also have the option of using a springboard to provide a more explosive start for the mount. You may use either bar to mount, but most gymnasts prefer to use a combination of both.

If the coach wishes to spot you, he may stand on either side of the bars but not be-

tween the rails. He may not touch the equipment while spotting.

One of the most popular mounts of medium difficulty is the *glide kip* (Diagram 69). This trick also serves as a vital connecting part for interior sequences. Without using a kip, it would be very difficult to maintain continual motion on the bars. Although the kip is not considered extremely difficult compared to many more spectacular tricks, it probably demands as much arm, shoulder, and abdominal strength as any bar movement. The glide kip can be performed from a number of different positions. It can be executed on the upper bar and lower bar, from one bar to another bar, with or without a twist, and facing either direction.

Movements on the Bars

The sequences between your mount and dismount can be composed of an endless variety of swinging parts, in combination with releases, regrasps, kips, and twists. In general, a movement with a half twist or less is considered to be of medium difficulty, while a movement with a full twist or more is of superior difficulty.

One of the more easily recognized tricks is the *flying hip circle into an eagle catch* (Diagram 70). The key to performing this trick is to spring off the low bar as high as possible while maintaining a horizontal body position. Some gymnasts are capable of lifting this movement almost to the height of the upper bar. If you lift only the upper body and not your legs, it will result in an improper lift of the body in a vertical position. The horizontal body lift is always preferred in an eagle catch.

You can perform variations of all the standard bars movements on the eagle catch; for example, you can perform facing either direction, or you can include a half or full twist. The only limitation of the eagle

DIAGRAM 70. The flying hip circle into an eagle catch.

catch is that it must be performed from a hip circle off the low bar.

Dismounts

Dismounts from the uneven parallel bars can be very exciting. One of the most spectacular is the *hecht* (Diagram 71), which is most often executed from a circle off the low bar. However, it can also be performed off the upper bar, facing either direction.

Performed from the low bar, it is considered a medium-difficulty movement; performed from the upper bar, it is superior. In either case, the addition of a half twist or more guarantees a superior rating.

On this movement height is very important. Simply sliding off the bar to the ground is not satisfactory. There must be a definite lifting action that allows your body to lift well above the bar in moving outward

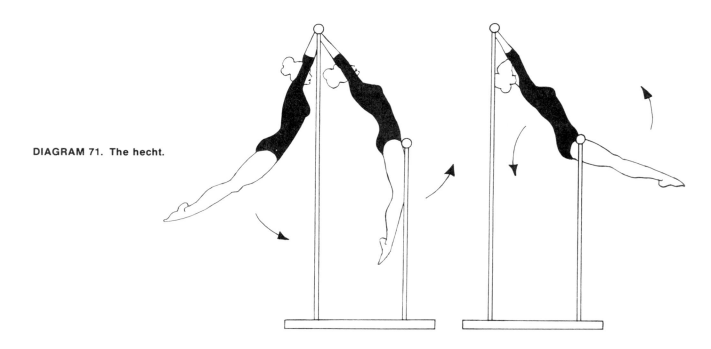

DIAGRAM 71. The hecht.

and away from the equipment. Although a possible variation of the hecht is to straddle the legs in flight, keeping the legs together is generally considered more difficult. As with all dismounts, you should give special consideration to mastering a secure landing.

Somersaults are also performed as dismounts, either from a support or hanging position from the hands. An important res-triction forbids you from somersaulting from a stationary standing position on the bar. All dismounts must be performed in combination with a hand release (Diagram 72).

VAULTING

Vaulting requires leg strength for running and for making an explosive jump. The basic techniques for women's vaulting are

DIAGRAM 72. Somersaulting dismounts from the bars.

the same as in the men's events, with two significant differences: (1) the horse is lower for women and (2) women vault over the width rather than over the length of the horse. The official horse height for women is 47¼ inches. Vaulting is less demanding and requires fewer tricks than the other three women's events, but the vaulting

score is just as important to the all-around performer as the score for the far more difficult balance beam, floor exercise, and bars events.

Should the gymnast require a spotter, the coach may be positioned only on the descending side of the vault. He may not stand between the springboard and the horse, touch the horse, or signal or speak to the gymnast during her performance. If he assists the gymnast, there is a 2.0 point deduction.

Evaluation

Women are required to perform two vaults, with a brief rest between them. A gymnast may perform two different vaults or make the vaults identical. The higher score of the two is her official score. The first vault is scored before the gymnast makes her second attempt. On the basis of the score awarded for the first vault, a gymnast can then decide whether or not to perform a different vault.

In case of misjudgment during the *run*, as the approach is called, the gymnast is allowed to take a second run, providing she has not touched the horse. If she contacts the horse in any manner, her movement is classified as a vault. An extra run is allowed only once for the two vaults.

The gymnast must announce her vault before she begins. She will often do this by selecting the vault number (posted at the far end of the runway) according to the International Table of Vaults and showing the card to the judges. Performing a vault other than the one indicated results in a 0.5 point penalty. An alternate method is to give the name of the vault to the head judge.

Before receiving the starting signal from the head judge, a gymnast may position the springboard in a suitable location. The distance of the board from the horse will vary with each type of vault and with the stature of the gymnast. In order to guarantee sufficient pre-flight, the board is usually placed a distance greater than the length of the gymnast's body.

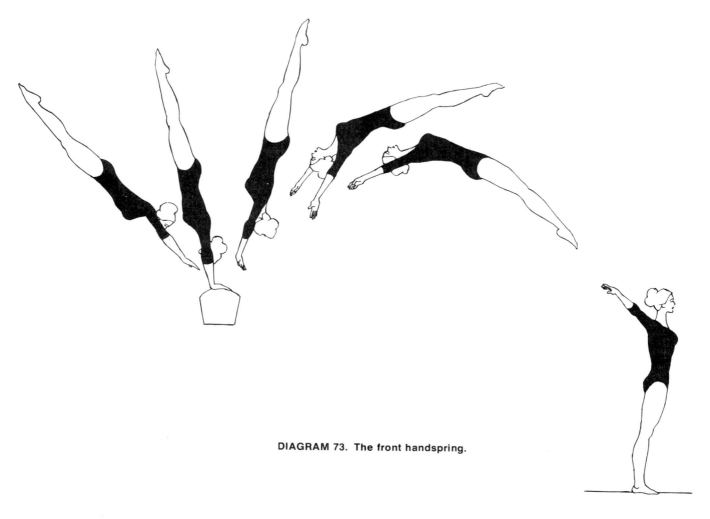

DIAGRAM 73. The front handspring.

DIAGRAM 74.   The giant cartwheel on, three-quarter-turn off.

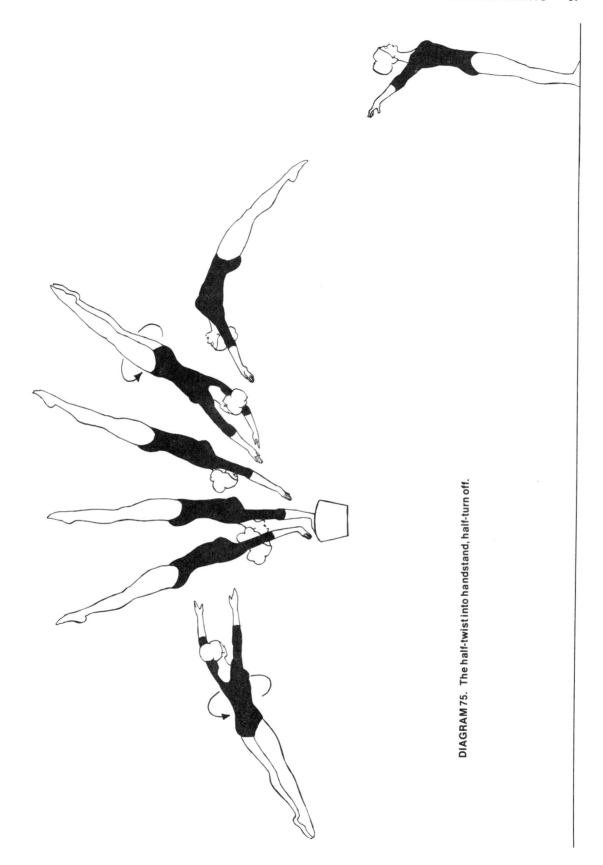

DIAGRAM 75. The half-twist into handstand, half-turn off.

To receive the highest number of points (10.0 rating) a vault must satisfy the following requirements:

1. The run must be strong and quick.
2. The takeoff must be explosive.
3. In the pre-flight segment, the gymnast must display quick, rising heels.
4. The hands must reach the horse quickly.
5. Repulsion off the horse (with the hands) must be immediate.
6. The trajectory of the vault must rise higher on post-flight than pre-flight.
7. The landing must be secure, without an extra step or hop.

The most common error is neglect in the post-flight phase (Diagram 36, Chapter 4).

A great number of vaulters demonstrate greater height in getting to the horse than on leaving the horse. This difficulty is usually due to the narrowness of the area provided for hand placement on the horse. Timing of proper hand placement on the narrow horse body becomes very critical.

Vaults in national and international competition are rated from 7.0 to 10.0 points. Since most 10.0 vaults are within the capabilities of an advanced gymnast, very seldom will an attempt be made to perform anything lower in value.

Vaulting Movements

The Yamashita (Diagram 37, Chapter 4) is as popular with women gymnasts as it is with men. A slight variation of the Yamashita is the standard front handspring (Diagram 73). It differs from the Yamashita in that your body remains straight throughout the entire vault, without any pike whatsoever. Again, extra height on post-flight is necessary to establish proper trajectory.

Twisting vaults are usually performed from the basic handspring position. You may wonder why a gymnast would select a twisting vault, generally considered more difficult, when there are vaults without twists that already have 10.0 rating. Actually, twisting vaults have a better chance of scoring higher, since the judge is allowed to make fewer deductions on vaults showing greater risk. Even though two vaults may be awarded the same preliminary rating, it stands to reason that a vault demonstrating more risk should receive fewer deductions for a minor error.

I must caution you, however, that this more lenient approach by a judge will seldom account for more than one- or two-tenths of a point. Risk is recognized, but never to the extent of overlooking proper technique. Never make the mistake of attempting to perform a movement beyond your capabilities.

Two of the more popular twisting vaults are the *giant cartwheel on, three-quarter-turn off* (Diagram 74), and the *half-turn into handstand, half-turn off* (Diagram 75). Both require a firm body position. When executing these vaults, keep your body stretched out while maintaining good form.

AMPLITUDE . . . is demonstrated by this performer, who is lifting her legs
to their maximum limits. Developing amplitude takes years of careful conditioning
and proper exercise.

chapter 6
CONDITIONING

No athletic activity puts a greater assortment of muscles to work than gymnastics. With each new trick learned, a different set of muscles is put into play. Joints in the hips, shoulders, and limbs are called upon to flex and extend to their maximum limits.

Proper conditioning is dependent upon a good workout program. Becoming a proficient gymnast is not something you do overnight. It takes time and patience. In order to progress at a reasonable rate, you must maintain a regular, daily workout schedule.

THE WARMUP

Conditioning should begin with a suitable warmup session before each workout, as is necessary in all sports. Gymnastics also demands that the shoulders, back, and hips be stretched and properly conditioned (Diagrams 76 to 79). This preliminary stretching process is necessary before each daily practice. Failing to stretch properly allows the joints to lose the flexibility so necessary for correct execution.

Most gymnasts spend from 20 to 30 minutes warming up. Usually the warmup routine begins with a light bit of running to get the blood circulating. The gymnast then concentrates on limbs, hips, and shoulders, loosening and stretching each area separately until a desired comfortable degree of flexibility is attained. This degree of flexibility will vary greatly among gymnasts. For all but a very few gymnasts, improvement in flexibility is a major objective. A gymnast usually avoids heavy, muscular exercises during the warmup, since they are a waste of energy.

After the preliminary stretching, the gymnast begins to work on the equipment. He begins by executing some of the more basic movements. These gradually condition his joints and muscles. The warmup period is seldom a quick process. And for a gymnast who may still be sore from the pre-

DIAGRAM 76. Touching the floor, an exercise to develop hip flexibility.

DIAGRAM 78. The back bend, an exercise to develop back flexibility.

vious day's workout, the warmup can be a painful ordeal.

THE WORKOUT

Working out three to four hours each day five to six days per week is about average for the serious competitor. And, unlike in most seasonal sports, this schedule must be carried out year-round, with a brief two- or three-week layoff during the summer.

The most productive time of day for practicing is between 2:00 and 6:00 P.M.

Earlier in the day, it is hard to get started, and in the evening hours body reactions are starting to slow down.

As a means of cooling off after a hard practice, most gymnasts will finish their workout by performing individual tricks. Tapering off from full routines to individual parts is a good way to avoid fatigue.

GENERAL CONDITIONING

A gymnast must develop split-second timing, complete concentration, good balance,

DIAGRAM 77. The split, an exercise to develop hip flexibility.

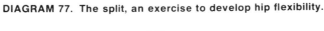

DIAGRAM 79. Stretch forward at a hyperextended shoulder angle, to develop shoulder flexibility.

and strength. Obviously, you will never develop these qualities unless you follow a carefully planned health program. As with all sports, you can't give your best if you smoke or drink, or if you fail to eat nutritionally balanced meals.

Resting properly is just as important as working hard. Take a day off at least every week. A day off gives your muscles a chance to recover from the minor strains accumulated during the week. It is also essential to get a good night's sleep before each day's practice.

As you can see, a person who wants to become a good gymnast must make it almost a full-time job. But the rewards are great, too. You will have the sense of well-being that comes from being in top physical condition and the confidence that comes with being in complete control of your body.

appendix: judging

The role of a judge is complex and laborious. Total concentration and a complete knowledge of the Federation of International Gymnastics (F.I.G.) Code of Points are essential. The F.I.G. Code of Points for men and women is available through the United States Gymnastics Federation, Box 4699, Tucson, Arizona 85717, and is the basis for much of this chapter.

Becoming a judge takes many years of personal involvement and study. Competitive gymnastics experience is a common prerequisite. The judge must also have a complete knowledge of the rules, right down to the minor points of evaluation. National as well as international judging clinics are held to certify judges on their ability to officiate at local, regional, national, and international competitions.

COMPETITIVE RULES FOR MEN

The evaluation of optional exercises, with the exception of vaulting, takes place on the basis of four factors:

1. Difficulty (11 parts)	3.40 points
2. Combination (requirements)	1.60 points
3. Execution (form and correct technique)	4.40 points
4. Bonus Point for R.O.V. (risk, originality, virtuosity)	0.60 points
TOTAL	10.00 points

DIFFICULTY (3.4 points)

To attain the highest possible score for difficulty, the exercises on floor exercise, pommel horse, rings, parallel bars, and high bar must contain the following individual parts:

5 parts of lower difficulty, called *A parts*
5 parts of intermediate difficulty, called *B parts*
1 part of superior difficulty, called a *C part*

These A, B, and C parts are given the following values:

A part = 0.2 point × 5 = 0.8 point*
B part = 0.4 point × 5 = 2.0 points
C part = 0.6 point × 1 = 0.6 point
Total points for difficulty = 3.4 points

---

*(In explanation of the 0.8 maximum point allowance for A parts, it should be noted that if the gymnast fails to demonstrate a minimum of five A parts, an additional 0.2 points is subtracted from his score for combination.)

Deductions for difficulty may not exceed 3.40 points. If a gymnast demonstrates the minimum number of A, B, and C parts named above, he has the right to a maximum score of 3.40 points for difficulty. If a gymnast accomplishes more than the prescribed C parts, but fewer B parts, the additional C parts automatically are counted as replacements for the missing B parts. C or B parts may also be used to replace missing A parts. On the other hand, if a C part is replaced by a B part only, 0.20 points are deducted for the missing C part. This means that a B part will partially replace an omitted C part. But under no circumstances may an A part be used to even partially replace a B or C part. Deductions for missing A, B, and C parts are as follows:

For each missing A part	0.20 point
For each missing B part	0.40 point
For each missing C part	0.60 point

COMBINATION (1.60 points)

The *combination* (construction) of an exercise is judged according to the following guidelines.

1. *Floor exercise* must form a harmonious and rhythmical whole. It must include parts of balance, hold, strength, jumps, kips, handsprings, and somersaults. All available floor space in all directions should be used.

2. *Pommel horse* exercises must be composed of clean swings without stops. Movements should include undercuts of one leg, circles of one and both legs, and forward and reverse scissors, of which at least one must be executed twice in succession. Double leg circles must be predominant, and all three parts of the horse must be used.

3. *Rings* must involve movements alternating between swing, strength, and hold parts, without swinging of the rings. The exercise must have at least two handstands, one performed with strength and another performed from below the rings with swing. Furthermore, the exercise should contain one strength or hold part of B or C value, in addition to the handstand performed with strength.

4. *Parallel bars* must consist of exercises showing swing, flight (releases), and hold parts. Although strength parts are not required, they are allowed. The exercise must have a B or C part executed under or over the bars in which the grips are released and regrasped simultaneously.

5. *Horizontal bar* (high bar) requires primarily swinging parts without stops. The minimum requirements for combination are a dorsal hang or grip and at least one combination involving a simultaneous release and regrasp of the bar with both hands.

Deductions for combination factors can be made up to 0.30 points for each error.

EXECUTION (4.40 points)

Execution errors can be made with the foot, leg, head, arm, hands, and body positions with regard to holds, stops, and touching the equipment. General execution errors and corresponding deductions are:

1. An unintentional spread of the legs, each time	up to 0.30
2. Touching the equipment accidentally, each time	0.20 to 0.50
3. Unintentional stops or hesitations, each time	0.20 to 0.50
4. In case of a definite sit down, or fall	0.50 to 0.70
5. Walking in a handstand (0.10 per step)	up to 0.50
6. Strength parts that are executed with swing, or swing parts that are executed with strength, are penalized	up to 0.30
7. The time duration for hold parts	2 seconds
Nonobservation of this time duration will bring the following deductions:	
A. If the hold is only ½ second	no credit
B. If the hold is only 1 second	0.20
C. If the duration of a hold part is held more than 3 seconds overtime	up to 0.30
8. On the rings:	
A. Handstand with bent arms	0.20 to 0.30
B. Touching straps with the arms	0.20 to 0.30
C. Cross with not completely horizontal arms	up to 0.50
D. Front lever not completely horizontal (body)	up to 0.50
E. Swinging of the rings (cables)	up to 0.30
F. Unwanted fall from a handstand	up to 0.50
9. On floor exercise:	
A. Lack of harmony, rhythm, and flexibility, deduct each time	up to 0.20
10. On pommel horse:	
A. Lack of amplitude in double leg circles	up to 0.30
B. Scissors below head height	up to 0.30

11. For general errors:	
A. Handstands not held vertically (straight)	up to 0.30
B. Hasty transitions from one part to the next	up to 0.30
C. A small step or hop on the landing (dismount)	up to 0.20
D. Poor posture before or after the exercise	up to 0.30
E. Support of hands, or one hand, on the floor, kneeling, sitting or other falls	0.30 to 0.50
F. Incorrect form or poor posture when being elevated to the horizontal bar or rings by an assistant	up to 0.30
G. Undisciplinary and unsportsmanlike behavior	up to 0.30
H. Falling from the apparatus to the floor	0.50
I. Form breaks: bent knees, flat feet, crossing feet, or an undesirable spread of the legs, each time	up to 0.30

VAULTING

Evaluation of vaulting is according to four factors:
1. Difficulty (rating assigned to each vault)
2. Pre-flight (from the board to the horse)
3. Post-flight (from the horse to the mat)
4. Form and execution (throughout entire vault).

Vaulting errors are penalized in accordance with the following:

1. *Pre-flight* before the minimum 20 degrees (when executing a far end vault)	up to 1.00
2. Insufficient *post-flight* after pushoff	up to 1.00
3. Poor position of the feet, arms, legs, head or body; or parting of the legs in flight	up to 0.30
4. Touching the horse with the feet, knees, and other parts of the body	0.20 to 0.50
5. Bending of the arms when pushing off	0.30 to 1.00
6. Bent knees when not called for	up to 1.00
7. If a gymnast runs more than 20 meters	up to 0.30
8. Pre-flight below horizontal (when executing a near end vault)	up to 1.00

COMPETITIVE RULES FOR WOMEN

Optional competition for women is evaluated on the basis

of 10.0 points for a perfect routine. Evaluation is based on:

1. Difficulty	3.0 points
2. Originality (1.50) and composition (0.50)	2.0 points
3. Execution and amplitude	4.0 points
4. General impression	1.0 point
TOTAL	10.0 points

DIFFICULTY (3.0 points)

To obtain full difficulty (3.0 points) on floor exercise, balance beam, and uneven parallel bars, an exercise must contain the following individual parts:

3 superior difficulty parts valued at	0.60 each
4 average difficulty parts valued at	0.30 each

The above difficulty requirements are limited to the following restrictions:

1. A maximum of 1.2 may be earned for any number of medium parts.
2. At no time may a superior difficulty be replaced by an average difficulty.
3. Elements of superior difficulty may be substituted for elements of average difficulty.

ORIGINALITY AND COMPOSITION (2.0 points)

Appropriate deductions are assessed for absences of the following elements:

1. Lack or excess of one type of movement	0.1 to 0.2
2. Masculine movements or masculine appearance of an exercise	up to 1.5
3. Lack of originality	up to 1.5
4. Repetition of a compulsory part with the same movements before and after	up to 0.3
5. Combinations too difficult or unsuitable for the gymnast	up to 0.5
6. Performing all superior parts at the beginning of the routine	up to 0.5
7. Failure to use the entire area	up to 0.5

EXECUTION AND AMPLITUDE (4.0 points)

Faults and deductions:

1. Unintentional bend in the arms, legs, or body, each time	up to 0.5
2. Unintentional spreading of the legs	up to 0.5
3. Landings without suppleness	up to 0.2
4. Touching floor slightly with one or two feet	up to 0.2
5. Slight loss of balance on landings	up to 0.2
6. Lack of continuity between movements, each time	up to 0.4
7. Falling on the floor or apparatus	0.5 and above
8. Overall jerky execution	0.5 and above

GENERAL IMPRESSION (1.0 point)

1. Lack of lightness	up to 0.5
2. Lack of dynamic expression	up to 0.5
3. Lack of beauty, grace, and elegance	up to 0.5
4. Lack of fluency	up to 0.5
5. Lack of body coordination	up to 0.5
6. Lack of suitable posture	up to 0.5

NEUTRAL DEDUCTIONS

Frequently penalties will not fall into the common categories. Such neutral deductions pertain to the following faults:

1. Fall from the balance beam	0.5
2. Fall from the uneven parallel bars	0.5
3. Physical assistance by the coach	1.0
4. Coach speaks to the gymnast (or reverse)	0.5
5. Gymnast stops due to personal fault (floor exercise)	0.5
6. Somersaults on floor under head height	up to 0.2
7. Music not following regulations of only one instrument	1.0
8. Stepping outside the floor exercise area, each time	0.1
9. Showing turns in only one direction on the balance beam	up to 0.3
10. Combinations and movement too advanced for the gymnast	up to 0.5
11. Over-use of one particular skill	up to 0.5

VAULTING

Women's vaulting is evaluated on the basis of four factors:

1. Difficulty (rating assigned to each vault)
2. Pre-flight (from the board to the horse)
3. Post-flight (from the horse to the mat)
4. Form and execution (throughout the entire vault)

COMMON FAULTS AND PENALTIES

1. Insufficient pre-flight (between board and horse)	up to 1.0
2. Bending the arms in support	up to 1.0
3. Touching the horse with the feet	up to 0.5
4. Insufficient post-flight	up to 0.5
5. Landing on floor heavy and uncertain	up to 0.2

6. Touching hands to the floor	up to 0.5
7. Support of both hands on the floor	0.5
8. Landing with support of body against horse	0.5
9. Landing on seat	0.5
10. Aid of the coach on landing	0.5

COMPULSORIES

For further clarification it should be restated that the compulsories are a complete set of routines separate from the optionals.

In national competition for men and women, compulsories are evaluated on the basis of execution only. Since difficulty and combination are prefixed factors in compulsories, it is not necessary for the judge to take these factors into consideration.

In spite of the fact that compulsories are generally composed of fewer difficulty elements than we normally see in optionals, the total score possible on each event remains at 10.0 points.

glossary

Aerial: A movement in which the gymnast turns completely over in the air without touching the floor with his hands.

Air sense: The ability to sense one's position in the air; an awareness of position.

All-around gymnast: A performer who works all events.

Amplitude: The maximum possible extension or lift in an upward and outward direction.

A part: A movement of lower value.

Apparatus: The equipment used for gymnastics.

Arch position: A curved, hyperextended position in which the body is bent backwards.

B part: A movement of intermediate value.

Circles: A pommel horse movement in which the gymnast rotates his body around the pommel horse while holding both legs firmly together.

Club swinging: A gymnastics event in which two wooden dumbbells were swung simultaneously. The event was discontinued in the early 1950s.

Code of points: The international book of rules for judging of gymnastics competitions.

Combination: The construction of an exercise; the proper sequence of the various movements and requirements throughout a routine.

Compulsories: Predesigned, required routines that contain specific movements.

C part: A movement of superior value.

Crash pad: An 8-inch (or thicker) soft mat used as a safety device for practice. The mat is not allowed for formal competition.

Difficulty: The effort and risk inherent in a movement.

Difficulty rating: The F.I.G.-assigned value for a movement with regard to effort and risk.

Dismount: The final movement in a routine, in which the gymnast goes from a piece of equipment to the floor.

Dorsal grip: A movement performed with the high bar held behind the back of the gymnast.

Eleven-part requirement: The minimum requirement for all men's events except vaulting. The requirement includes five movements of lower value (A-parts), five movements of intermediate value (B-parts), and one part of superior value (C-part).

Emery cloth: A type of sandpaper used for removing excess chalk that accumulates on the equipment.

Execution: The manner of performing movements with regard to foot, leg, head, arm, hand, and body position.

Exhibition: The act of performing a routine during competition with the understanding that the scores received will not be counted. Such a routine is performed for experience only.

Fall: An unintentional landing on the mat.

F.I.G: Federation of International Gymnastics.

Floor mats: A soft, padded mat used as a safety device to absorb the jarring action on landings. Usually one to two inches thick.

Flexibility: The quality of suppleness in the joints.

Flying rings: A former competitive gymnastics event that allowed the gymnast to perform while the rings were set in motion. The initial swinging action was created from a push provided by an assistant. This event was discontinued in the late 1950s.

Form: A position in which the legs are held straight and firmly together, with the feet and toes pointed.

Full difficulty: Fulfilling all requirements of risk as well as combination.

Grips: Handguards.

Hanging position: The act of hanging from the equipment by the hands.

Head judge: One of the four judges. His responsibility is to check that all four scores flashed by the judges are within proper range. In the event of an obvious discrepancy, he calls the judges together for a consultation.

Height: The elevation of a trick above the apparatus or floor.

Hop: The act of stepping forward with two feet in an effort to regain balance during the landing phase of a dismount.

Intermediate swing: An extra swing or part of no value.

International style: The correct manner of performing a gymnastics movement.

Inverted position: A position in which the feet are directly over the head.

Kip: A movement in which the gymnast moves from a hanging position (below the equipment) to a support position (above the equipment).

L-position: A position in which the body is bent forward 90 degrees at the hips.

Landing: The final position on the mat after completing a dismount.

Landing mat: A mat about 4 inches thick that is usually placed in the landing area for dismounts from the apparatus.

Layout position: A position in which the body is kept straight or slightly arched during a movement or a still position.

Leg work: Movements performed with the legs apart on the pommel horse. *Also called* single leg work and scissors.

Lineup: The listing of competitors in order of participation for each event.

Mount: The first movement in a routine, in which a gymnast gets up onto the equipment.

Official timer: A person responsible for timing the length of routines.

Open competitions: Meets open to any athlete who fulfills the basic requirements for that particular competition.

Optionals: Routines designed with movements of the gymnast's own choosing.

Part: A single movement or skill.

Part of no value: A simple skill unworthy of receiving even an A-part rating.

Pass: A sequence of movements in floor exercise that move in one direction.

Pike position: A position in which the body is bent forward at the hips while the legs are kept perfectly straight.

Pommels: The wooden handles located on the top side of the pommel horse body.

Post-flight: The portion of a vault from the horse to the landing mat.

Qualifying meets: Competitions set up to qualify individuals and teams for the national championships.

Pre-flight: The portion of a vault from the springboard to the horse.

Repulsion: The pushing action of the hands in lifting the gymnast off the horse body in vaulting.

Requirements: Certain skills, positions, or releases that must be included within a routine.

Rip: A piece of skin torn away from the palm of the hand.

Rope climbing: A former competitive gymnastics event for men, which involved climbing a height of 20 feet with only the hands. The event was discontinued in the late 1950s.

Rosin: A hard, brittle resin that is applied to the soles of gymnastics slippers to improve traction.

Routine: A full set of gymnastics skills performed on one event.

Runway: The narrow approach area used by the gymnast to initiate a run for vaulting.

Sequence: A series of movements.

Somersault: A complete 360-degree rotation of the body in the air.

Specialist: A gymnast who performs on only one event.

Split: The act of spreading the legs as wide apart as possible. Correct execution is to have both legs spread 180 degrees apart, stretched forward and backward.

Spotter: An assistant who is positioned near the apparatus to aid the gymnast in case of a fall.

Springboard: The takeoff board used for vaulting and performing mounts on parallel bars and uneven parallel bars. *Also called* a Ruether board.

Stop position: A pause in the execution of a movement.

Straddle position: The act of spreading the legs sideways as wide as possible.

Strength part: A movement performed with strength.

Superior difficulty: The rating given to a movement that demands enormous effort and involves extreme risk.

Support position: A position in which the gymnast supports his body weight with his hands and arms, above the equipment.

Swinging part: A movement performed with a swinging action of the body.

Trajectory: The curve of a vault as it moves from the board, over the horse, and onto the landing mat.

Transitions: Connecting parts joining tumbling sequences in men's floor exercise.

Trick: A movement or gymnastics skill.

Tuck position: A position in which the gymnast bends his knees and holds his legs tightly against his chest with his hands.

Tumbling: A former competitive event for men and women in which the gymnast was expected to perform four tumbling passes down a 60-foot tumbling mat. Tumbling was discontinued as an event during the early 1960s.

Twisting: Turning on the longitudinal axis of the body.

Vaulting zones: Two sections of the horse body designated for hand placement.

Warmup: The process of loosening up the muscles and joints of the body.

index